UNTOLD MILLIONS

UNTOLD MILLIONS

Positioning Your Business for the Gay and Lesbian Consumer Revolution

GRANT LUKENBILL

HarperBusiness

A Division of HarperCollins*Publishers*

HarperCollins books may be purchased for educational, business, or sales promotional use. For information please write: Special Markets Department, Harper Collins Publishers, Inc., 10 East 53rd Street, New York, NY 10022.

FIRST EDITION

Designed by Irving Perkins Associates

Library of Congress Cataloging-in-Publication Data

Lukenbill, Grant.
   Untold millions : positioning your business for the gay and
lesbian consumer revolution / Grant Lukenbill. — 1st ed.
      p.   cm.
   Includes bibliographical references and index.
   ISBN 0-88730-699-3
   1. Gay consumers—United States.   2. Lesbian consumers—United
States.   3. Marketing—United States.   I. Title.
HC110.C6L85   1995
658.8'348—dc20   95-24276

---

95 96 97 98 99 ❖/HC 10 9 8 7 6 5 4 3 2 1

For my kind and gentle brother, Ralph Lukenbill. And in dear memory of Gary and Kelvin—I miss you both.

CONTENTS

Photographs follow page 116.

ACKNOWLEDGMENTS

▼ ▼▼▼▼▼▼▼▼▼▼▼▼▼▼▼▼▼▼▼▼▼▼ ▼ ▼ ▼

This book reflects the personal contributions and professional commitments of hundreds of persevering and trusting people. For listening, strategizing, and conducting historical, groundbreaking research on gay and lesbian Americans as consumers, I am most grateful to the wise and talented people at Yankelovich Partners, Inc.—particularly Rex Briggs for his team spirit, critical thinking, and formulation of the psychology of disenfranchisement.

Although too numerous to mention individually, I want to thank all the publishers, editors, writers, and salespeople at daily newspapers and gay and lesbian weekly newspapers and publications across America who contributed their time, opinions, research, databases, and Rolodexes to this work. Numerous gay- and lesbian-owned small businesses have made important contributions as well, and I am grateful for their time and professional courtesies.

For constructive criticism of my ideas and arguments, mature debate, and encouragement from the beginning of this project, I'm particuarly indebted to my friends and trusted confidants Adrian Milton, David Winters, and Michael Gast. I also want to acknowledge the contributions and personal—at times critical—support I have received from Dorothy Atcheson, Sidney Casares, Chad Edwards, Amy Ginsberg, Neil Goldman, Jay Hill, David Kraft-Schutte, Nan Liebowitz, Stan Redfern, David Rephun, Bob Riner, Lois Sheeler, Lisa Tritico, Steve Turtell, Steve Walton, and Jimmy Wilmore. I thank Bill Dobbs for always reminding me of my roots.

For providing their professional suggestions and gentlemanly support I want to thank Frank Mount and Adrian Zackheim. Likewise, I am grateful to my agent, Charlotte Sheedy, for her important work and especially for her belief in me and this project.

For their editorial contributions to the early manuscripts and for providing competent advice on this book's structure and impor-

▼ ▼

tance, I have editors Virginia Smith and Jane Loeb to thank. I am equally indebted to Suzanne Oaks, my friend and editor at HarperBusiness—particularly for her patience, dedication, and attention to detail. I wish to acknowledge my sincere appreciation for Janet Kvamme, my bibliographer, for her keen sense of history—and especially her extraordinary work in association with James Briggs Murray at the Schomburg Library in Harlem. Extensive thanks are due as well to my trusted friend and art buddy, Patrick Arena, for his patience and loyal editorial and research assistance, and to Ron Niemann whom I love most for his unswerving commitment to spiritual friendship and a sense of humor too twisted for words, but well appreciated during the burning of the midnight oil.

For inspiration and endless reams of newspaper clippings, letters, pictures, phone calls, and who knows how many hours spent in libraries, I want to acknowledge the editorial contributions and shrewd—at times ironic—political insights of my brother, Ralph Lukenbill.

And of particular importance, I want to acknowledge the specific interviews, personal contributions, and priceless little gems of perspec-. tive brought about during sometimes brief but important discussions with Dan Baker, Matthew Bank, Amanda Bearse, Alan Berube, Stephanie Blackwood, Jay Blotcher, Howard Buford, Dennis Colby, Bob Craig, Dan Dailey, Rob Davis, John Dellassandro, Michael Denneny, former New York City Mayor David Dinkins, the Honorable Tom Duane, Martin Duberman, Murray Edelman, Stuart Elliott, Paula Ettlebrick, Mildred Gardner, Stephen Gendin, Timothy J. Gilfoyle, Barbara Gittings, Michael Goff, David Gold, Barbara Grier, Will Guilliams, Harry Hay, Mark Horn, Frank Kameny, Michael Kaminer, Jonathon Ned Katz, Robert Kilgore, Paul Kowal, Richard Laermer, Dorr Legg, Steve Levenberg, Phyllis Lyons, Del Martin, Deacon McCubbin, Ed Mickens, Kendall Morrison, Ann Northrop, Roz Parr, Ron Owen Partners, Clarance Patton, Dell Pearce, Victor Ponte, Tom Reilly, Alan Roskoff, Gabriel Rotello, John Sabulis, George Sancoucy, Luc Sante, Michael Shively, Francis Stevens, Sean Strub, Donald Suggs, Andrew Sullivan, Harry Taylor, Nancy Webster, Irvashi Vaid, Jeff Yarbrough, and numerous people at the International Gay and Lesbian Archives, the Lesbian Herstory Archives, the New York Advertising and Communications Network, Rivendell Marketing, the

▼ ▼

staff of the 1994 Gay Games, Stonewall Twenty-Five, and the Wall Street Project.

For their unconditional love and financial support (especially when the going got rough), I'm eternally grateful to my family, to Bill and Lois Wilson and their family, and to my father, David Lukenbill—your basic all-around great guy.

CHAPTER 1

▼ ▼

YOU CAN TAKE IT TO THE BANK

Marketing has just changed. Things are going to get very different, very quickly.

The time is nearing when lesbian mothers will promote bleach and fabric softener on national television. Gay male sports figures, sponsored by tennis shoe companies, will soon be emerging as spokespersons for the prevention of violence in our nation's public schools.

Sound unbelievable? Believe it. The signs are all around us.

It is time to get prepared. If you don't, you or your company will miss out.

It doesn't matter if you are a business owner, employer, stockholder, or an interested employee or consumer. It doesn't matter if you are gay, straight, lesbian, bisexual, single, divorced, separated—with or without kids.

A bullish, fast-moving train of economic momentum is thundering down the track. And it means invigorating economic opportunities for businesses and social institutions—both large and small, rural and urban.

We are not talking about a social trend. This is a marketplace revolution—serious, multifaceted, and destined to reorganize customer landscapes in consumer product and service industries across the country. Gay and lesbian consumerism, and the spectacular developments it is spawning, is already affecting much of America's commercial media imagery. It is impacting corporate hiring practices in the workplace and even the commercial buying habits of heterosexual Americans.

1

▼ ▼

Up until the last few years, the effects and influences of these changes have been extremely subtle, playful, even covert. But gay and lesbian consumers have long seen them everywhere—most recently in the way heterosexual men's erotic publications play up "lesbian sensitivity," and in the way Hollywood has pushed gay male stereotypes in television and film all through the twentieth century.[1] What is interesting, is that there has always been an economic motivation behind the depiction and positioning of unrealistic homosexual ideals in the commercial marketplace: basically because there has always been a payoff.

For instance, just after the beginning of the twentieth century, during the early years of (what is now called) the mental health field, psychiatrists seized upon the opportunity to pontificate about the "sickness" of gay and lesbian people—even legitimizing their stature by making supposedly learned arguments about the dangers of their serving in the military.[2] Of course, that argument is still with us, but the days of finding an automatic payoff at the expense of gays and lesbians are fading away fast. As is the demand for the archaic stereotypes of lesbians and gay men—because the days of an exclusively heterosexual model of commercial consumption are dead.

A dynamic infusion of economic opportunity for American business is now invading the entire commercial spectrum—one that is more historic than the appearance of gay male walk-on parts in soap operas and more substantive than the subjugation of lesbians in straight male erotica: the power of the gay and lesbian consumer dollar and all that it represents. This power can mean increased revenue for the business you own or work for. It can solidify a shrinking sales database in a company's direct-marketing efforts. It can prop up a brand's sagging performance in highly competitive geographic areas. It can even bring credibility to a corporate image in need of one or make a company more attractive for prospective employees, partners and associates, or lucrative government contracts—even mergers.

Soon, a sparkling presence will be widely apparent—one by which even some gays and lesbians will be completely surprised. And it is growing right out of their own community: the gay and lesbian consumer revolution in America. This revolution will ultimately result in a seismic shift in popular culture. The effects are already proving unavoidable for every large corporation and company with a product to sell or an employee to hire. And according to Stephanie Blackwood, an associate publisher with *The Advocate,* the oldest national gay and lesbian news publication in America, "people [in business] who acknowledge the moral obligation to the gay community" are the ones who will ultimately be regarded as the leaders.

What is coming specifically is a cataclysmic change in the spending patterns of millions of American consumers—gay and lesbian as well as heterosexual. For many companies, the entire way of doing business will alter significantly as a direct result of gay and lesbian buying power and its indirect commercial influence.

Does this sound far-fetched? Consider what's already going on.

"Big Business Boosts Effort to Win Share of Gay Market" read the *Wall Street Journal* banner headline this past May immediately following the National Gay and Lesbian Business Expo at New York City's Jacob Javits Convention Center. "'Half of the 225 exhibitors were mainstream companies, up from about one-third of a much smaller group last year,' said Steven Levenberg, show manager."[3]

At American Airlines, Rick Cirillo was recently appointed "Sales Manager for the Gay and Lesbian Community" and his business card lists him with that title.[4] According to Cirillo, this came about based on a proposal that he himself presented to the senior VP of Passenger Sales regarding the growth and importance of the marketplace. Comments Cirillo, "We [at American Airlines] are happy to be leaders in this area; we allow our gay and lesbian customers' to obtain bereavement fares [reduced flights in the event of the death of a domestic partner], and our frequent flyer miles can be used between gay and lesbian domestic partners" (a benefit only available on some airlines to married heterosexual couples).

Gay and lesbian buying power is now recognized as such a commercial and economic force that it is affecting decision-making at Hill and Knowlton Public Relations, American Express, Nike, Calvin Klein, Revlon, AT&T, Time Warner, Continental Airlines, NBC News, Home Box Office, IKEA, and General Motors. These and other companies are pondering all the social nuances and marketing opportunities that are being brought about by this new age of racial and sexual diversity, identity consciousness, and marketplace hyper-segmentation. Marketers from Madison Avenue to Silicon Valley are discussing and negotiating these exciting new realms—from hospital corporations and health clubs in the South

▼ ▼

to the Biltmore Hotel in Los Angeles and the American Marketing Association in New York City.

In the recording industry strong niche sales among lesbian consumers can no longer be denied. According to author and New York radio personality Vicki Starr, one of the first out lesbians in American radio, "for years in the country music business there was this belief that women country music artists don't sell. Well now those people are realizing otherwise."

The word is out with the all the major television networks, with Miller Beer, the Republican Party, and the animated halls of Disney; it is impacting media buying for Naya, Evian, and Perrier waters; it is changing employment and insurance policies across the country; it is even stirring in the Catholic Church and affecting politics and rhetoric within the inner sanctums of the Vatican.

Changes in television are apparent in both cable and broadcast realms. "Home Box Office has been topnotch in every way in terms of policies; they are very understanding when it comes to benefits for gay and lesbian employees," says Richard Mayora, account executive for HBO.

And according to Joe Decola, a producer with NBC News, "We are certainly covering more gay and lesbian news now than we were five years ago—in fact, dramatically more. And I would even say somewhat more than just three years ago. In the country overall, there's a cultural change taking place, there are just more people out today—out in media and in the workplace—that's certainly the case at NBC News—and it all contributes to a growing sense of awareness."

Awareness indeed. Savvy business leaders everywhere now agree, gay and lesbian market segments are finally heating up. As is the competition for the brand loyalty, the cultural relationships, and of course, the profits. And the trend is clearly moving swiftly and solidly toward inclusivity.

According to J. Walter Thompson partner and associate research director Tony Incalcatera, "Gay and lesbian consumers have come to expect a lot of solicitation from American business. This is now requiring that really smart marketers—meaning cost-efficient and effective marketers—are going to have to start building and helping to transmit specifically focused messages that reach the greatest cross section of consumers—that means communicating inclusivity to gay and lesbian consumers as well as other minorities. Not always

▼ ▼

an easy thing to do. But if advertisers forgo sexual inclusivity, they are going to find themselves in an upstream battle and eventually facing overly diluted brand loyalty."

This book presents the first broad-scale accounting of contemporary gay and lesbian consumer culture in America. It provides a fundamental program for understanding gay and lesbian consumers, who they are, and how they think.

It is about how business will become stronger, more ethical, and more profitable by appealing to an exciting new consumer that is eager to buy but quick to see through smoke and mirrors, hollow rhetoric, and misguided marketing. Hundreds of millions of dollars in industry profits are now at stake for American businesses that position themselves to appeal to these highly specialized consumer market segments. By the turn of the century gross sales in products and services aimed directly at gay and lesbian consumers will be measured in the billions. Hundreds of major corporations know this as well as thousands of small businesses—and they are all making plans in anticipation of continued growth.

According to Steve Bolerjack, vice president and co-director of a recently formed gay and lesbian marketing group at Hill and Knowlton Public Relations in New York City, "We are now focusing and increasing our activity in anticipation of new business in the gay and lesbian marketplace both in New York and Los Angeles. And we intend to begin pitching new business in this area because we simply see a great deal of potential. Our objective is also to better help our existing clients market their products and services to the gay and lesbian community. We want to help them approach the community as an important niche market. Businesses today would be wise to begin targeting and considering the gay and lesbian community as a viable market that deserves consideration in the overall mix of business and market planning."

This advice is echoed by Michael Adams, senior editor for *Successful Meetings*, a trade magazine that follows American business meetings and incentive travel management: "People [in business] are shifting their attitudes. Diversity is now a big issue and the good news is that there are movements going on to include sexual orientation language and consciousness among [the meetings industry's] professionals." Adams was recently asked to speak on gay and lesbian issues for the International Association of Exhibit Managers.

▼ ▼

According to him, this would have been unheard of in the 1980s. Yet it was in the early 1980s that gay and lesbian consumers were on the cutting edge of the information superhighway already communicating over the Internet through *soc.motss* (Members Of The Same Sex), which boasts in excess of 70,000 readers—and that's not counting the now jam-packed bulletin board forum at America Online founded in 1991 by Gays and Lesbian United Electronically (GLUE).[5]

Clearly, the time is now to convince gay and lesbian consumers they should be online and on board with your company—that they should be loyal to your products and your services. The road map is in your hand.

Getting to Know What You're Looking At

To begin to understand gay and lesbian consumers is to begin to understand how they have been economically closeted within a marketplace that has been, for the most part, "heterosexually oriented" for much of this century.

Only in the last twenty years—and especially during the past five—has a truly sophisticated sense of awareness about image and image messaging begun to emerge in marketing with regard to sexual identity. The boundaries continue to change as more companies learn how to push the envelope of commercial aesthetics and social tolerance in pursuit of wider market shares within their respective industries. This dynamic is true across the board: from fashion, advertising, film and television, and the science of direct marketing to the positioning of beer brands, recorded music, and presidential election campaigns.

America is entering the golden era of gay and lesbian visibility. And because gay and lesbian Americans are no longer willing to exist within social closets, they are also no longer willing to conform to the confines of yesterday's marketing paradigms. Erin McHugh, an advertising creative director with Franklin Spier Agency in New York City, agrees, stating: "I think it's fair to say that the history of advertising and the marketing of imagery in general has been largely centered around heterosexual archetypes." That is what is changing. Today gay and lesbian people are out—not only as individuals, but as informed consumers who expect companies to communicate a sense of awareness and comprehensive understanding of who they are, and who they are not.

These important developments among gay and lesbian consumer groups are requiring savvy marketing professionals—and the corporate leaders who listen to them—to begin to facilitate and nurture the amplification of sexual diversity within the landscape of commercial imagery. In other words, to allow a wider, more realistic range of America's spiritual and emotional character to be explored in relationship to sexual orientation, personal identity, and how importantly they relate to product marketing.

Ultimately, this requires business to adopt an understanding and ability to interface company management policies with gay and lesbian social standards and consumer ethics. It also requires that advertising leaders revisit their notions of what constitutes "appropriate" visual and stylistic coding in the creative development of visual arts. It requires that new things be tried, that boundaries be pushed and that new messages be communicated to express inclusiveness, understanding, and validation of America's emerging pansexual culture. Which brings us to the discussion of gay and lesbian market messaging.

Coming Out with the Code

All around us in popular culture is code—social code, sexual code, image code. Code is about creating "double-speak." Some of it is obvious; some of it is crafty. Advertising in particular is all about code and the sending of pluralistic messages. So is political posturing, which makes use of code with the so-called sound bite. In the response to our "sound-bitten" information age, the news media attempts to break down the code—but all too often ends up creating more code—because news itself is a product, requiring its own standard of coding.

Code is about the sending of messages, manipulating perception, and the calculated planting of ideas between the lines and behind the scenes of information imagery. It is about the shrewd and persistent use of cunning language in our overly commercialized mass culture. It happens in politics. It happens in marketing. It also happens in our living rooms.

When code is used constructively to reach gay and lesbian consumers—meaning metaphorically, and in the proper cultural context—it can be the advertiser's single most important tool: a subtle

▼ ▼

communication formula to lock in brand identity and communicate a broad sense of individual inclusion across gay and lesbian consumer groups as well as heterosexual ones. Unfortunately, the vast use of code in modern free enterprise is usually more exploitive and disruptive rather than supportive and nurturing of the individual.

For instance, when code is used by the food and beverage industry, we see it in the aggressive marketing of fat-free products and the subtext suggestions of desirability that comes from being thin, which whispers, "Don't be like those people who have a weight problem." Modern food and beverage advertising is loaded with sexual suggestion and the promise of physical satisfaction, all in an effort to push processed, mass-produced foodstuff commodities. It is particularly apparent in the presentation of desserts and low-fat products, but is even used within the presentational context of "premium" cat foods. The way in which many edible products are currently being photographed in the 1990s, stirring, oozing, dripping, and steaming across consumers' lips, tongues, and fingers, would have resulted in disgust and outrage just a few years ago. Today, food and hunger are coded as something beyond a mere primal desire. They are presented in lewd-like contexts designed to create a delusional promise of hyper-satiation. It is all coding, though, designed to play on a number of American's insecurities about need, desire, and an oversexualized sense of fulfillment and personal satisfaction about life in modern times.

The irresponsible use of coded messaging by modern corporate market forces runs through the entire twentieth century and is now more pervasive at every level of society than ever before in the history of capitalism. It is widely responsible for the amplification of minority stereotyping—particularly with regard to gay and lesbian Americans. And it is obviously a contributing factor to the spread of violent and hedonistic ideas among youth and the breakdown of societal structures and numerous minority cultural institutions.

As Cornell West wrote in *Race Matters,* on the challenges specifically facing black cultural institutions in America:

> Corporate market institutions have contributed greatly to their collapse. By corporate market institutions I mean that complex set of interlocking enterprises that have a disproportionate amount of capital, power, and exercise a disproportionate influence on how our

▼ ▼

society is run and how our culture is shaped. Needless to say, the primary motivation of these institutions is to make profits, and their basic strategy is to convince the public to consume. These institutions have helped create a seductive way of life, a culture of consumption that capitalizes on every opportunity to make money. Market calculations and cost-benefit analyses hold sway in almost every sphere of U.S. society. The common denominator of these calculations and analyses is usually the provision, expansion, and intensification of *pleasure*. . . . The reduction of individuals to objects and pleasure is especially evident in the culture industries—television, radio, video, music—in which gesture of sexual foreplay and orgiastic pleasure flood the marketplace.[6]

When code is reduced to its skeletal structure, it is always about selling ideas and communicating positions. It's simply part of free enterprise. Sometimes it is used to shock, grab attention, or create divisive discussion. It is mixed, subliminal, at times disingenuous, and at times validating—but rarely completely trustworthy. Most recently it was used by Burroughs Wellcome in their $25 million advertising campaign designed to get people (particularly gay men) to start taking the drug AZT. The campaign—which ran widely in gay publications and in outdoor advertising placed in gay neighborhoods—focused on health and the importance of getting tested for HIV, which is a responsible message. But the coded subtext was about getting people to take the drug AZT should they test positive for the HIV virus.[7] This was done before the efficacy of the drug's ability to prolong life was widely accepted among gay men. It is still contested today.

Call advertising code what you like—sinister *double-speak*, corporate public relations, brand loyalty development, product identity and positioning, relationship marketing, or consumer-object affection, it is all profit-based marketplace messaging. And it is all used to get you to change your mind about something relating to your purchasing behavior, regardless of reality, and often in denial of solid facts, personal intuition, and basic human nature.

Of course, not all advertising and marketing is coded or needs to be. Copywriting used in direct-marketing letters and customer loyalty campaigns (such as frequent flyer programs and best customer campaigns) often rely on direct and up-front communication as a way of creating an attractive, crystal-clear image in the consumer's mind leading ultimately to the purchase of a product.[8] But even the

▼ ▼

imagery used to accompany direct-mail letters is often laden with more than one message. And when it comes to the proliferation of mass imagery and messaging in the external commercial market-place, you can confront any management executive or brand manager of nearly any popular product in America about its advertising motivations and psychology and you will get even more code. Spin. Public relations. The prepackaged package.

Few mainstream companies or advertising agencies successful at attracting and keeping gay and lesbian consumers for their clients will admit that any kind of code has been their mainstay. Of those that will, even fewer will elaborate on the details. But being able to use code, specifically in the pursuit of gay and lesbian consumers, is one of the most important tools that has worked up till now. Some of America's better advertising writers, artists, and photographers know exactly what they are doing when it comes to using code. Many of the executives who hire them may not always recognize or specifically acknowledge this as a talent, but their ability to exploit the possibilities of code is often the competitive edge that shows up in their portfolios, gets them hired, and ultimately produces imagery that gets consumed by the masses.

Most consumers would be hard-pressed to identify or crack code whenever it shows up in marketing imagery. And certainly few heterosexual consumers (and businesspeople) are aware of just how often they are being bombarded with gay and lesbian advertising code—an awareness that gay and lesbian Americans call "gaydar,"a kind of sixth sense, an intuition about gender-specific sensuality, artistic sensibility, and cultural archetypes.

Some gay and lesbian imagery, in varying degrees, shows up in commercial media and is often called the "androgynous look" in advertising shop talk. But it reads as code to gay and lesbian consumers—many of whom are insulted by its use if it is sprinkled around too carelessly.

Two important facts surround the use of code. The first is that same-sex advertising code (imagery that can potentially be perceived by a consumer as gay/lesbian or straight) makes it into broad cross sections of American advertising whether it is done on purpose or not. The second is that same-sex imagery does in fact help sell products, precisely because it can be taken so many ways without being seen as necessarily single or married, exclusively straight, or exclusively gay or lesbian.

Communicating an unspoken suggestion of gay/lesbian code in images produced by the image business is something most spokespersons for Madison Avenue and its clients don't jump to the microphone to talk about. There are usually one or two simple reasons: the appointed individuals speaking on behalf of the company might be too embarrassed or too ignorant of actual gay and lesbian market issues to discuss the subject with authority, or they want to protect their prized secrets on how they came to attract and keep their gay and lesbian consumer following.

Patrick Lehman, a New York-based visuals and image design consultant who has advised everyone in advertising and fashion, from Calvin Klein to Kmart, has very strong ideas about what informs and makes the use of code effective when targeting gays and lesbians—particularly when it comes to them as clothing and fashion consumers:

> *Twenty-five years ago you had five magazines in America. We sold ourselves on a single culture. Today our culture is broader, longer, and more diverse. People who read* Vibe, Esquire, *or* The Advocate *may still read a fitness magazine, an industry trade publication, and the local newspaper because you can't get everything in one place anymore. So as a designer I have to do something to cut through the noise. And when it comes to gay and lesbian people, I find that they'll always buy 'clever,' even though it may not be exclusively aimed at them. Generally, I think that any kind advertising in any industry that is hip, ironic, or contains a little attitude, sarcasm, or bitchiness is what gay people will click on to. Often gay and lesbian people have a certain bitterness from being oppressed by mainstream society. So by being on the outside looking in, for so long, many of them actually revel a little in things that are really 'arch' or a little on the sneering side.*
>
> *But that's only part of the picture. Good compelling imagery also has to be exciting, electric, and stimulating to different people for different reasons, but it all has to happen at once—as an ensemble of feeling. It's hard to always boil it down to a specific formula. And it doesn't always have to be sexually suggestive. But turning up the heat and widening the panorama of sexual tension is definitely something everybody tries to do, and the unfolding of more gay and lesbian consciousness is simply part of that evolution in marketing. Not everyone wants to admit it, but that's exactly what's going on.*

Advertising professionals on the account side of the business are especially nervous when it comes to the issue of homoerotic sexual tension—particularly in relation to their tactical strategy and posi-

▼ ▼

tioning of a product against an aggressive competitor. This is because gay and lesbian publishers and advertising directors—and especially gay and lesbian employees at large advertising agencies—have known for years that there is no industrial or commercial playing field littered with more social taboos, corporate minefields, and political booby traps than the gay and lesbian marketplace. For instance, just getting a senior-level manager at a large advertising agency to sign off on the actual paperwork required within the company to place advertising buys in gay and lesbian media (for any client) has never been an easy task. In fact, many clients would enter the gay and lesbian consumer market if it were not for the timidity of their agency of record. Yet, almost as if to overcompensate, many agency creative departments routinely produce some of the most homoerotic imagery imaginable. More of it was seen throughout the 1980s than the entire decades of this century combined. Consumers see it—both gay and straight. But up until recently, as Lehman acknowledges, nearly everyone has been afraid to talk about it.

Indeed, for years fashion advertising never appeared in gay and lesbian magazines, but the marketing firms and ad agencies that produced and placed imagery for the fashion industry did everything but acknowledge that gay people were part of the overall mix of consumers being targeted through the mainstream. A cursory glance through any *GQ* or *Cosmopolitan* during the last quarter of this century bears testament to the fashion and advertising industry's ongoing fetishistic affair with same-sex imagery.

This trend toward sexual inclusiveness continues to this day and is now apparent in nearly all industries that make use of mainstream advertising. And, finally, more and more media buys are being made in gay and lesbian publications. Today American advertising, and media imagery in general, abounds with more mixed signals and subtly woven homoerotic imagery—for both men and women—than ever before.

This imagery does not exist as a conspiratorial agreement between model, photographer, stylist, and media buyer. It is now part of an overall understanding and acceptance of a changing consumer marketplace. Perceptive, leading-edge companies recognize that lesbians and gay men are part of their sales base and can, in fact, be reached through the mainstream if approached with the right messaging and an appropriate level of sensitivity, so as not to

▼ ▼

distract or dilute heterosexual interest. This is especially noticeable in the increased and highly sophisticated depiction of a more generalized sense of sensuality, which is often blended with a liberal attitude about human nudity.

According to Vincent Boucher, a New York creative director and fashion stylist with ten-plus years' experience in the development of some of America's most important visual imagery,

> *Advertising is sexier than it was twenty years ago—today it can cut both ways, playing to straight audiences and gay audiences at the same time. Today there's a broadening of scope about who's going to be 'brought in' by advertising. It's really an evolution that started in the 1980s with photographers, and now the body itself has become such a totem. Although nudity by itself does not have a gay connotation in our society, it can still be used to pull in a gay audience—as can an ironic stance, for instance, or a kind of humor that is wry and urban. When designers get together to do a shoot we don't sit down and say, 'OK, is this going to appeal to a gay audience?' It may get commented on from time to time but it's really now just part of the package. I don't think 'gay' has to be discussed, but I do think people are thinking about it now. It's an accepted part of the job that you have to appeal to all audiences.*

Indeed, all it takes to see what Boucher is talking about is a simple look around the country at the way we have come to accept more and more sexualized advertising imagery over the past two decades. It is widely apparent in dozens of consumer industries— particularly in the marketing of fashion, men's underwear, alcohol, blue jeans, cigarettes, automobiles, bath soap, and fabric softener.

The liquor industry has become particularly adept at signaling its desire to communicate to all consumers: straight, as well as gay and lesbian consumers. Consider a recent Dewar's Scotch advertisement that plays on a number of suggestions about sex and the taboo of discussing male anatomy. The advertisement was particularly unbelievable—even to gay men (see photo insert). Interestingly, it plays to all audiences. It also toys with the brazen without being too suggestive of behavior or sexual fantasy.

Underwear has also seen a lot of play lately. For instance, women make up a sizable proportion of many of the American male's underwear buying decisions in this country. But what other male group was Calvin Klein playing to when he blazoned the near-nude body of the handsome and muscular young Marky

Mark across the sides of buses and billboards all over America?

It is highly unlikely that many heterosexual men were sexually turned on by a young white male with perfect washboard abdominal muscles wearing double-digit-priced Calvin Klein underwear. On some level they might have fantasized about being as young, physically fit, and attractive as Marky Mark and therefore more attractive to women. But there were no women in many of the shots of him. So was the heterosexual male supposed to take a leap of faith in the fantasy? This kind of aggressiveness has certainly not been the trend in selling beer, sports cars, or certain colognes to men. Nor has it ever been the approach used to sell products in much of the advertising seen in *Sports Illustrated*—a decidedly male-focused publication.

So who else was buying the underwear besides all those heterosexual men who aren't married or in an intimate enough relationship to receive the gift of underwear from a woman?

And what was the symbolism behind Marky Mark's bashful smile and his hand being placed between his legs?

Translation: Yes, I'm attractive to many American women—but in a bashful sort of way. And, yes, I know you (gay) men find me attractive, but I'm straight and you can't have what I got. So I'll literally create a boundary here between you and me and my sense of maleness by covering myself with my hand. Oh, you can continue to look, because I'm paid to let you. Just be sure and pick up a package the next time you're in the store and thinking of me.

According to Lehman, who was working for Calvin Klein at the time, Marky Mark "was a perfect universal object of desire, he was a fantasy for many gay men because he represented the unattainable man, being straight, yet for women he was young and cuddly; the adorable boylike man you want to hug."

Brilliant advertising? Yes. And brilliant use of multilevel coding as well.

Calvin Klein underwear is still the underwear of choice among tens of thousands of gay men across America—most of whom, it is safe to say, do not have many women buying their undergarments for them. Interestingly, the Calvin Klein underwear campaign that followed the Marky Mark campaign did incorporate a female model undressing a male model—but only after it was ascertained that a trend could be reinvented with underwear by appealing to a certain market segment of male youth through mixed messaging.

▼ ▼

How about a recent advertising campaign for Virginia Slims cigarettes? Remember the one that showed two young women staring into each other's eyes while sitting very close to each other at a sidewalk cafe? They both had big smiles on their faces—as if they were really into each other's company or perhaps had just shared a intimate secret. The ad read, "The most important thing about a break is who you take it with."

In downtown New York City, a Guess Jeans billboard advertisement shows three GQ-looking white men sitting in the front seat of a convertible looking over their shoulders toward the camera, which is behind the car. Guess Jeans does not think that heterosexual men are necessarily attracted to young men who ride together three at a time in the front seat of an automobile. Indeed, there are probably few straight men in America—especially that young—who would automatically choose to ride in the front seat of any car with two other guys when there is plenty of room in the back—especially if they are single and in a convertible. Interestingly, though, it is something that gay men might do. The point here? The construction of the photo is subtle enough to say something to everyone—regardless of sexual orientation.

Madonna was one of the first major performers to blanket America with sexual code—code used specifically to appeal to the entire panorama of sexual expression—and this was especially obvious to gay and lesbian consumers. Many of the artists and industry professionals Madonna works with are gay or lesbian, and a healthy portion of her talent developed and became popular as it emerged from the downtown New York club scene—which is very gay.

Madonna learned about and utilized a real part of her experience with gay and lesbian culture as a way to propel many of her more popular artistic ideas forward. It is no wonder that she is widely adored by gay men and particularly respected by many American lesbians for her independence, courage, and self-actualization as a woman.

Also consider the humor of Roseanne and her "lesbian kiss" episode with Mariel Hemingway. It was one of the most watched shows of the television season and a near perfect and direct use of marketing code. It resulted in an increase in audience share and a continued loyalty to Roseanne and her character among a broad cross section of television viewers. Including such scripting insured gay and lesbian viewership, and it communicated a sense of social

▼ ▼

"brazenness" during prime time, when the most profit stood to be realized.

In case you haven't noticed, there is a cross-dressing fad in teenage-oriented commercials for everything from bubble gum and soda pop to basketball shoes and breakfast cereal.

This is not so much sexual code as it is cultural code—an acceptance of a diluted "camp sensitivity." It is a zany but effective way to develop brand identity and loyalty while simultaneously presenting a product in a lighthearted way that young, puberty-age consumers can relate to but not feel sexually threatened by.

If you are now saying to yourself, "Oh puh-leeze," you might want to consider that that expression itself has long been a stereotypical lament among older gay Americans. It was infused into popular culture by gay situation comedy writers in New York and Los Angeles in the 1970s and is now routinely used by everyone from Joan Rivers and David Letterman to Camille Paglia, Larry Kramer, schoolteachers, and politicians.

Seeing Is Believing

Today gay-and-lesbian-oriented imagery and social colloquialism—both purposefully coded and directly communicated—is everywhere in American culture. This is because gay and lesbian consumers now represent an amalgam of diversity, ethnicity, individualism, and values, all extrapolated in many different social allegiances.

The imagery behind these allegiances exist right now, right under the nose of every American consumer, in our media, advertising, popular music, arts and entertainment, magazines, and television commercials. But because the gay and lesbian marketplace has been so specialized and so elusive, yet so much a coded—and closeted—part of the American commercial fabric, it has up until now gone virtually unnoticed by the heterosexual majority.

This is what is changing.

Every major bookstore in every major city across the United States now has a gay and lesbian section. Bookstore managers have learned that gay and lesbian consumers are constituting a larger and larger portion of their regular customer base.

There are now more nationally distributed, nonerotic, advertiser-

▼ ▼

supported gay and lesbian glossy magazines on America's news-stands than there are fashion magazines for men.

Out, Genre, Ten Percent, Men's Style, Deneuve, Girl Friends, Frontiers, The Advocate, and even *Details* (for gay and straight men) and *POZ* (for people living with HIV) all continue to enjoy growing circulations and a steady increase in total advertising pages all through the 1990s.

Some of the most successful television presentations in America, including, *Roseanne, Frasier,* and the PBS airing of *In the Life* and Armistead Maupin's *Tales of the City,* benefited enormously from their decision to incorporate a clear level of visibility for gays and lesbians.

MTV now transmits the music, words, images, metaphors, and symbols of a gay- and lesbian-infused culture on the hour every hour into 70 percent of American households—every single day. They even used Roseanne as their host during the 1994 MTV Music awards. The music video sensations of megastars Elton John, k.d. lang, Melissa Etheridge, the Indigo Girls, Madonna, Prince, Michael Jackson, Sting, and others all garner strong gay and lesbian followings based on their socially conscious lyrics and sensitivity to a cultural diversity that embraces all groups.

In addition, popular male performers like Elton John, female rock-and-roll sensation Melissa Etheridge, country music's k.d. lang and Fox Television's *Married with Children* star Amanda Bearse have all come out as gay or lesbian. And each has enjoyed an immediate increase in their ratings, popularity, record sales, and ability to communicate a moral sense of political and social responsibility to their fans by virtue of being more open about who they are and what their work can be about.

Of course, entertainment industry producers are all thrilled as well. They know something dramatic is happening—something they can all take to the bank—which is why more films like *Priest* and *Boys on the Side* are now being marketed by Hollywood executives who sense the changing tide in consumer demand. The same is even true in the television now being aimed at adolescents. And what is really exciting is the level of sensitivity and responsibility with which the subject matter is being dealt.

A successful reality-based series on MTV called *The Real World* included a gay male character, Pedro Zamora, who was gay, HIV positive, and in a relationship with another man. When Pedro died in late 1994, it was telling how many straight and gay and lesbian fans felt the loss.

Pedro had been featured on the cover of *POZ*, a competently edited and distinctively designed magazine aimed at everyone concerned or affected by HIV and AIDS. *POZ*, of course, has a strong leaning toward gay and lesbian editorial content, but includes a multitude of issues affecting all Americans dealing with AIDS. In the MTV show, Pedro and his boyfriend were portrayed as they had really lived their lives, with all the issues surrounding being gay, living with HIV, and interacting with a heterosexually dominant society—presented sensitively, frankly, and unsensationally.

In addition, the interior furnishings for the show were provided by IKEA in exchange for promotional announcements. IKEA was the first home furnishings company to run a TV advertisement showing two gay men buying a coffee table together. Savvy gay male teenagers are quite aware of the MTV *Real World*–IKEA connection.

Even *The New Yorker* has become demonstrably gayer since the editorial reins were given to former *Vanity Fair* miracle worker, Tina Brown. As better and more frequent articles about gay and lesbian culture have begun to appear in the *The New Yorker*, so have more subscriber cards from gay and lesbian readers. The June 1994 cover (see photo insert) demonstrates just how attuned Ms. Brown is to what her magazine can now take to the bank.

Martina Navratilova is a celebrity model for Apple Computers. An Apple computer advertisement showing Martina—a gay woman—holding her PowerBook while standing next to wide receiver Art Monk—a straight man—has appeared on the inside front cover of numerous magazines, including *OUT*, one of America's most popular gay and lesbian general interest publications. Many lesbian students, technicians, and executive professionals are more prone to buy Macs than other laptops. Now you know why.

Direct response is especially prominent in the gay and lesbian marketing explosion. It offers many companies a way of testing the waters before going into a high-profile campaign through print media. Even gay and lesbian consumers are not always aware that many of the catalogues they receive in the mail were sent to them specifically because they are believed to be gay or lesbian by companies doing direct marketing.

Most recently, gay/lesbian-owned clothing and product cata-

▼ ▼

logues have begun to appear across the country. One of the largest players in the gay and lesbian direct-marketing arena is the *Shocking Gray Catalog*. *Shocking Gray*, like *The New Yorker*, has learned how to position itself to gay and lesbian consumers with an increasingly competitive design approach.

Levi Strauss, *Larry King Live*, Benson and Hedges cigarettes, Miller Beer, Calvin Klein, Donna Karan, Tommy Hilfiger, Madonna, RuPaul, Marky Mark, Phil Donahue, Oprah, and Sally have all learned that gay and lesbian consumers and gay and lesbian money represent something new. You can do the same, and the time to start reordering your marketing perspectives is now.

Right now companies that want to obtain, keep, and develop better, more profitable consumer relationships with gay and lesbian Americans need to start learning, investigating, planning, and speaking to gay and lesbian consumers in a more contemporary way: in their language, on their turf, without corporate self-consciousness, and, most important, without the closeted economic straightjackets of the past. Communicating a company's awareness of gay and lesbian diversity positions a company as "socially conscious"—thereby increasing its brand loyalty among heterosexual consumers as well.

There will be some "transitioning" time as gay and lesbian imagery becomes less subtle, less coded, and more directly communicated in the mainstream marketplace. However, directness in advertising to gay and lesbian consumers is ultimately where the market is going. Companies that are willing to push the levels of "outness" and "directness" in their depiction of gay and lesbian sexuality, sensitivity, and emotion will be the ones known as the leaders.

One of the most beautifully produced advertisements aimed at lesbians exclusively comes from Olivia Cruises—a travel and vacation destination service for gay women. It unabashedly shows two women embracing on the beach in much the way Madison Avenue has stylistically portrayed heterosexual intimacy since the 1950s. This ad is a spectacular example of gay (more specifically, lesbian) advertising at its best—devoid of ambiguity and aggressive exploitation.

Of course, not all advertising can afford to be completely gay or lesbian. But, increasingly, neither can it afford to continue to act as if the world is completely heterosexual—or even asexual.

▼ ▼

Corporate America and its marketing representatives must learn to start speaking directly to lesbians and gay men—either through the responsible and cunning or subtle use of artistic and cultural coding as Calvin Klein and Madonna have, or through the completely out, no-holds-barred approach as Olivia Cruises, Oprah Winfrey, and MTV do. For those in business who refuse to do this, who refuse to explore these new realms in consumer marketing, who insist on remaining asleep at the wheel, the gay and lesbian marketing moment will utterly pass them by.

While there is a big payoff for conducting business with this genuinely new consumer marketplace, companies must accept that sexual diversity matters not only in the marketplace—but in the voting booth and in hiring practices.

The leaders are the ones who know that the future of gay and lesbian responsiveness to loyalty-driven advertising does promote corporate popularity, product identity, and long-term sales across many market segments, including those of heterosexuals—but only if their own house is in order. And only if an understanding of gay and lesbian consumers is dovetailed with a corporately communicated understanding of an entire spectrum of socially urgent issues.

The days of using heterosexually focused advertising themes exclusively to reach America consumers are over.

For the marketplace leaders, and those who want to join them, it is time to blast open the corporate doors of America's commercial closets. It is time to learn the facts about where the future of marketing to all consumers is going. It is time to put together a plan and get down to business—the kind of business you can take to the bank.

CHAPTER 2

▼ ▼

VISIBILITY

The New Politics of Profit

The life blood of our free enterprise system is a precious amalgam of liberty, equal opportunity, organizational independence, and perhaps most important—visibility.

Interestingly, it is the very same elements crucial to the survival of free enterprise that also make up the self-evidently held truths, morals, and building blocks of the contemporary equal rights movement among gay and lesbian Americans. Gay and lesbian freedom marches and pride celebrations are all about these same issues: liberty, equal opportunity, independence, organization, and visibility. Which is one of the reasons why the American gay and lesbian equal rights movement has gotten as far as it has today: its leaders have learned along the way how to make use of shrewd and compelling imagery.

In the early 1990s, commercial imagery in America began fundamentally changing across our entire media-drenched landscape: it was still shrewd, still compelling. But what changed was the fact that commercial imagery no longer had to be, without question, heterosexually affirming.

For over two hundred years, the mere acknowledgment of gay and lesbian people in American society was virtually nonexistent. This "nonexistence" was amplified in mainstream advertising and television media throughout the last hundred years. In many areas of the country, any allusions to same-sex affection were considered forbidden, even immoral—if not outright illegal.

Of those references to same-sex affection that did occasionally occur in television and film, most were of a highly stereotypical

▼ ▼

nature or were presented in less than accurate contexts—usually for the gratuitous consumption of what were assumed heterosexual audiences. Outside of the print advertisements seen in the gay and lesbian press or occasional tokenism in television dramas about "being different" or living with AIDS, accurate gay and lesbian imagery was rarely projected through mass media with any degree of fairness until the late 1980s.

Today, things are changing.

Even though the history of the gay and lesbian emancipation movement has been a fight for equal protection, the fair application of laws, public visibility, and the general public's acceptance of their moral legitimacy, as a group gay people are developing more than a political identity. They are in fact manifesting an economic and commercial identity as well as a cultural, philanthropic, and spiritual one.

What is developing is a more comprehensive gay and lesbian consumer *consciousness.*

Today, gay and lesbian consumers are more aware of the imbalances and inaccuracies relating to sex, affection, and emotion that persist in the mainstream's portrayal of their culture. They are aware of which religious figures embrace and support their causes and which ones do not. They know (with increasing comprehension) which business corporations are on their side and which ones are not. And perhaps most keenly, they have finely tuned levels of emotional and intellectual radar when it comes to the proliferation of inaccurate images of their contemporaries in commercial imagery.

One thing is for sure, gay and lesbian consumers see how visual imbalances and misrepresentations of gay people in a media-drenched society contribute greatly to the anti-gay violence in the neighborhoods where they live. They see how routine censorship of real issues and values ultimately breeds contempt and exacerbates ignorance in the populace—further preventing the passage of equal rights legislation and the establishment of anti-discrimination codes at the municipal level.

According to writer and veteran lesbian activist Ann Northrop, "There is a real misunderstanding of who we are. And then there's an assumption that we have made a choice—a sinful, disgusting, perverted choice that is about life style. There's a lack of understanding that we [gay and lesbian people] have an essential nature,

▼ ▼

and that the world is a diverse place sexually and that we have been discriminated against through misunderstanding and lack of education [of the public at large]."

In response to these imbalances, gay and lesbian consumers pay closer than average attention to nearly every public policy issue that comes up for review. They are also more likely to investigate corporate behavior—both inside and outside of the walls and grounds where businesses operate.

Gay and lesbian consumers have a heightened awareness and interest in corporate equal opportunity issues and are usually more aware than their colleagues of anti-discrimination policies affecting their position in the workplace. There is also increasing evidence that younger gays and lesbians vote more regularly and pay more attention to election-year political rhetoric.

Some of the most compelling evidence of this notion is chronicled in an important paper by Murray Edelman, Ph.D. and editorial director of the Voter News Service, a national consortium of the major television networks and the Associated Press. Edleman sights exit polls conducted during the 1992 presidential election by Voter Research and Surveys (VRS). The survey found that 71 percent of gay men and 69 percent of lesbians under the age of 45 voted, compared to 56 percent of straight men and 58 percent of straight women. What was striking was that most of the difference was found in the 18–29 range.[1]

Overall, the research data estimated the size of the national gay and lesbian vote to be about 3.2 percent. A *Los Angeles Times* poll conducted during the same time period was 3 percent—"An unusually close agreement for two totally independent surveys" states Edelman.

These findings shed interesting light on just how engaged America's younger gay and lesbian generation really is and how willing they are to identify themselves as being gay or lesbian in comparison to their more senior peers. It also helps explain why they are hypersensitive to the integrity of news broadcasts during the annual gay and lesbian marches for equal rights (held each June in commemoration of New York City's Stonewall Riots of 1969).

The currently maturing generation of gay and lesbian Americans is more visible and paying more attention to the business of conducting business and how it relates to their lives. And therein lies

▼ ▼

the opportunity for profit for companies that plan accordingly and with responsibility.

Strong Medicine for Corporate America

For America's companies to conduct business with gay and lesbian consumers today is to sooner or later confront the politics, challenges, and issues faced by members of that marketplace. Consumer goods manufacturers, corporate leaders, and advertising executives not willing to accept this reality would be better off closing this book, investing their marketing dollars in other niche segments, and hoping against hope that their clients and competitors don't continue reading.

Forewarned is forearmed. In the currently evolving, increasingly politicized and evidently forever-here-to-stay global consumer marketplace, gay and lesbian customers as a group are more aware, more in tune, and more willing to combine their politics with their discretionary spending for goods and services than any minority in American history. Moreover, their political consumerism is becoming increasingly more solidified under the current wave of conservatism in national politics.

This increased strength and heightened visibility draws even more attention to their potential worldwide importance as consumers in a changing marketplace. This visibility has captured the attention of airlines, credit card issuers, and foreign car manufacturers as well as domestic auto industry executives in Detroit, as witnessed by the recent advertising of Saab and Saturn in gay and lesbian magazines.

For those who have never heard it, hear the truth now: Gay and lesbian Americans are organizing in aggressively diversified ways—many of which, on the surface, may appear to have little to do with emancipation or marketing issues, but in the long run will change and redirect the way many of America's products and services are sold.

In the last eighteen months, gay and lesbian publications have begun focusing more closely on marketing, economic, and consumer issues. And more gay and lesbian nonprofit groups, political action committees, and activist groups have begun building coalitions around marketplace issues. Through gay and lesbian newspapers and magazines, on-line computer networks, and corporate gay and lesbian employee groups, gay and lesbian consumers are now

▼ ▼

tracking corporate America's relationship to them on a level unprecedented in free enterprise.

This heightened interest in the policies of America's companies both large and small is being rekindled as one of the most important trends among consumers both straight and gay—but it is currently being revisited and taken most seriously among gay and lesbian consumers. Such realities can be played to a company's advantage or they can result in a public relations nightmare that could take years to mend, unless proper action is taken when the opportunity presents itself.

That opportunity is now, particularly in light of the fact that acceptance of sexual diversity in American society is significantly more widespread than ever.

The following graph confirms the steady, systematic decline in prejudicial attitudes toward gay and lesbian people across the United States over the past fifteen years.[2]

"Would prefer not to be around gay people"

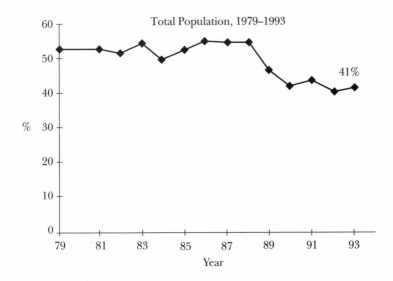

Source: Yankelovich MONITOR®

At the current rate of change as indicated above, it is clear that the majority of Americans across the country could be overwhelmingly in support of comprehensive equal rights for all gay and lesbian Americans by the turn of the century. Sooner or later there

▼ ▼

will be a federal statute on equality issues pertaining to gay and lesbian Americans in housing, employment, and access to spousal benefits. Any American corporation that does not at least have a policy banning discrimination based on sexual orientation will soon find itself among increasingly extremist company in the eyes of both gay and lesbian and heterosexual consumers alike.

Thousands of American companies are already (often at the advice of their legal counsel) finding themselves backpedaling on their outdated hiring policies and scrambling to put out routine public relations fires, all in the name of poor planning or pending lawsuits.

Regarding this specific issue, many businesses are realizing that this absolutely painless step (often a mere rewording of their employee manuals) translates to a wise, long-term investment eventually affecting their ability to attract loyal employees and sell stock and products. Senior-level executives that stand in the way of these changes in America's workplace ethics do so at their company's competitive peril.

Refocusing the Images

Whenever an attractive or newly supportive portrayal of gay men or lesbians occurs in a magazine ad, a newspaper article, a television situation comedy plot or direct-mail advertising campaign, rest assured that gay and lesbian consumers take notes, talk, and keep mental diaries. They gravitate at alarming speed toward any accentuation of the positive in media and commercial enterprise—which is what has been driving much of the strong brand loyalty trends tracked among gay and lesbian consumers for so many different products.

Until recently, wherever gay and lesbian Americans looked (at least outside predominantly gay neighborhoods) all they saw was imagery that could always be argued in ad agencies as being nothing more than heterosexually intended. Even fashion advertising aimed exclusively at men made use of the obligatory woman in the photograph's construction—much the way advertising made use of the token racial minority in the advertising of the 1960s.

Discerning which companies and advertising agencies were making use of any degree of code to quietly reach gay and lesbian consumers had to always be, on some level, deniable. It wasn't until the past few years that public relations departments began the spin that their advertising campaigns' visuals were aimed at all consumers in all walks of life.

Still, there were a number of shocking incidences throughout the past ten years that helped to rally gay and lesbian consumers toward a more focused analysis of products and services, marketing tactics, and the use of imagery in media in general. One of the more recent and most infamous examples, for Nut and Honey cereal, typified the advertising industry's history of ignorance and insensitivity to gay and lesbian Americans.

The commercial showed two cowboys placing guns next to the head of another who said the name of the cereal but was heard to utter the double entendre, "Nothing, honey." This suggested that he was gay but in a stereotypically prissy, effeminate, and therefore perverted enough way that they should protect themselves from his degeneracy by threatening him with murder via simultaneous gunshots directed to each side of his head.

Suggesting that gay and lesbian Americans are sick people, monsters who use prissy language that will contaminate the morals of the masses and are therefore worthy of death, is a classic strategy used by religious radicals and political extremists to this day. Still, it is almost unbelievable that such advertising actually made it on to national television within the past few years.

This may be a small example, but we must remember that modern communications culture is cabled, radio talk-showed, and Nightlined into a Larry King Live, Howard Sterned mass of lukewarm cynicism. Heterosexuality is still fighting to maintain its norm in the media, and a commercial like Nut and Honey's may seem mildly humorous to the uninformed, reminiscent of Old West skepticism, but it is seen by gay consumers as a frightening reminder of society's history of intolerance for the humanity of the homosexual public.

The frequent distortion or outright censoring of the "real" existence of gay and lesbian culture in modern life, in advertising imagery, in history books, and in the general media, combined with the occasional cultural bashing of gay and lesbian people through examples like Nut and Honey, has forced generations of gay and

▼ ▼

lesbian consumers to constantly make allowances and readjust-ments in their minds for heterosexual society's image-producing inaccuracies.

Even though times are changing radically, even though advertis-ing agencies, brand managers, television producers, and movie directors are beginning to be more inclusive of gay and lesbian cul-ture, another reality remains. In many areas of the United States, gay and lesbian consumers are not at all represented and are left with the option of completely rejecting mainstream culture (which many have) or subconsciously imagining themselves re-created in many kinds of American advertising campaigns, transposing their very wants, desires, values, sense of humor, and basic human feel-ings into the heterosexually intended affectations and communica-tions of modern imagery.

In other words, on some level they have to re-create the imagery to suit their own sense of perspective on the world. And of course, one's sexual orientation greatly affects one's perspective of the world.

For sure, different consumers experience varying degrees of fan-tasy and context recreation when exposed to different kinds of advertising. But with the exception of the ambiguous, ever-chang-ing world of fashion advertising, gay and lesbian consumers have to take most advertising in America a few steps further for it to have any relevance to their lives. A lesbian consumer admiring an ad in a women's business publication showing two women caught in the rain under one particular brand of umbrella, each with a hand holding the umbrella as they laugh and walk down a busy street, does not necessarily assume they are supposed to be straight friends on their way to work or out to do some shopping.

A gay woman might consider whether or not the ad was coded advertising aimed at her, or whether it was completely straight and therefore not inclusive of her or her lesbianism, or simply not well thought out and not the kind of umbrella she would buy anyway.

Of course, each woman judges for herself what appeals to her sense of individuality, femininity, and community involvement when she looks at a piece of advertising. Still, there's a lot wrapped up in the visual communication of advertising, and all the lines really blur when "same sex, sex appeal" becomes part of the pic-ture—whether it was intended to be there or not. What matters is

▼ ▼

whether the intention was to appeal to all women straight or lesbian, or whether it was simply a confused, off strategy execution, ill-
suited for the company and the product.

Marketers who are not asking themselves these questions about
the creative development within their advertising campaigns (and
making informed decisions based on proper research) are probably
costing their companies an indeterminable amount of money in
what could otherwise be increased sales volume.

Consider the leaps of faith—if not hilarity—that some gay men
take when their eyes glimpse the Marlboro Man cigarette billboards
(which are often conspicuously placed in gay neighborhoods).

The durable, red cotton-shirted man on the white horse, a stock
(largely heterosexual) American role model for strength, rugged-
ness, and solid western tradition, becomes everything from divine
comedy to exhausted sexual fantasy—especially for gay male non-
smokers: a middle-aged man in the middle of nowhere on a horse
with a nicotine habit trying to look straight?

Even Doublemint gum commercials tend to wax ludicrously
campy in the eyes of some gay and lesbian consumers—the smiles,
the hugging and laughing, the tongues, the rolling of the eyes—
even the writing is an absolute riot.

Consider the singsong lyrics, "Double your pleasure, double your
fun."

Sound too esoteric?

Don't forget the advertising that appeared routinely in fashion
magazines all through the 1970s and 1980s. Separate groups of
men or women were often seen walking abreast, together, or sepa-
rately. There was nothing to suggest they were married, dating, or
even heterosexual. But the ads were constructed in such a way
that gay men (*especially* gay men) could transpose themselves into
the pictures, as if they were the intended target. The models were
often posed in neighborhoods that looked like places where gay
men lived or would travel to. The men were usually never touching, of course, but the line of demarcation was always played as
close to the edge as possible. Same-sex affection was always hinted
at with an erotification of the "male look" opposed to the male
body. Eventually, some men began to be described as looking
"GQ"—a potential code word and clear radar detection device in
gay culture.

If all this unintended sexual cross-pollination of consumer imagery

▼ ▼

sounds like a potentially complicated psychographic dilemma for contemporary marketers and advertisers hoping to break into gay and lesbian market segments, it is. But it doesn't have to be an insurmountable one. Still, obstacles do have to be overcome. And differing products must be dealt with differently based on geography and a sense of what can be pushed to the proper limits and what must be left alone. Strategically, at the corporate and media managerial level, the questions must still be asked: Do we have gay and lesbian customers? Are we strengthening their loyalty to our products? What is our written policy regarding sexual orientation?

Probably most important, advertisers must consider all the damage that has been done over the years within their own industry. Has there been any history of insulting or neglecting gay and lesbian consumers by a company's competitors? Can this be used to a company's advantage? Is there a plan to insure that a company does not make the same mistakes that its predecessors or competitors have already made? Is the company really ready and dedicated to growing its customer base by entering a given gay or lesbian market segment?

If you consider the entire realm of images that cable television offers: live courtroom battles, child custody fights, murder followups and ambulance rides, hundred-dollar juicers and miracle mops, *Hard Copy* reruns, (heterosexual) soft-porn channels, variations on the ThighMaster, Cher-touted hair care products that "really aren't sticky,"—all on a par with "Deadbeat Dads Who Stalk the Neighborhood" or "OJ—Wife Basher AND Murderer?" on the next Oprah, it's not hard to see how easy it might be to construct and launch a gay and lesbian advertising campaign based on gay and lesbian "realism."

Such a campaign would easily sear through the gay and lesbian consumers' cynicism by avoiding the hype of modern commercial media. And it might innovatively communicate social consciousness to straight consumers as well as the gay and lesbian marketplace.

Still, a company should know what it is doing.

Putting First Things First

To understand, develop, and effectively market products and services to gay and lesbian consumers today requires an acceptance and intellectual empathy for the stark division of visual images in modern life

▼ ▼

between heterosexual culture and what has been stereotypically touted and visually exemplified on the evening news as "the gay lifestyle" (usually old shelf footage of two young gay men walking hand in hand out of a bar to the street of some assumed gay ghetto).

It also requires that business leaders develop an acceptance for the stark difference in the way gay and lesbian citizens are treated by the American justice system, the police departments, the medical community, and the education system. Serious marketers must have a firm grasp of the general political issues and the divergent perceptions between gay and lesbian consumers' view of the world around them versus that of heterosexuals if they are ever to forge new ground in the wide spectrum of gay and lesbian market segments. Further, they must consider all the issues as seriously as they do the development of their client's brand identities if they are to win profits—that is, compete—in the coming shift toward more openness in relation to gay and lesbian consumers.

The shrewdest of America's business leaders who genuinely want to embrace the profits that come from doing business with gay and lesbian consumers must be willing to allow the pioneering information contained in this book, trade magazines, and other relevant sources from within the gay and lesbian community to be burned into their consciousness if they are to begin to understand the context within which the American gay consumer exists, interacts, and ultimately accepts or rejects products, services, values, and ideals in modern culture. (Specific data and research in this area is discussed more in chapter 4.)

Gay Is Good. Big Is Not.

Americans bore easily when it comes to the media's handling of an entire host of cultural and political issues. And it is no wonder. All our major population centers have upwards of a hundred television channels of what many often complain amounts to nothing. Yet at any given moment, everything is available. The channel surfing continues.

We have it all. Test balloons on myriad issues are floated through the media daily by everyone from the Justice Department and the White House to the Home Shopping Channel and municipal governments. Senate, house, and presidential announcements are molded, timed, and delivered with simultaneous monitoring

▼ ▼

(which we hear later as a poll). And there is always a "fallback" position in case the numbers don't pan out as hoped.

What passes for news is often "information product" filtered through public relations firms. Publicists have shouting matches with columnists and talk show coordinators over who's getting the "exclusive."

We are lost in an endless barrage of commercial messaging designed to develop us into or keep us part of a particular market share. It all boils down to competition. And, of course, money.

Which is one of the main reasons why gay and lesbian visibility has appeared so quickly in the American commercial spectrum. And why it has also become so quickly embraced as a market dynamic.

It is the impact of the telecommunications explosion in concert with shrewd gay and lesbian political activism, and the insatiable thirst for a sound bite, that has solidly awakened America to a host of issues surrounding not only gays and lesbians but heterosexuals as well: blatant discrimination, physical and emotional abuse toward men and women in the armed services; AIDS, breast cancer, child abuse; religious extremism; and the ongoing health care crisis.

Last summer, a *Time*/CNN poll found that 62 percent of Americans questioned favor the passage of equal rights laws to protect gays and lesbians against job discrimination. Yet 65 percent of those same Americans also indicated that too much attention was being paid to such rights.[3]

The general feeling seems to be that we did the gays in the military thing. We watched the gays in Washington thing. We saw the gays in the Gay Games thing. As a television viewing public (and perhaps a nation) we've simply become bored with the issues surrounding the equal rights process for gay and lesbian Americans.

Interestingly, we're certainly not bored with gay and lesbian culture when it comes to investigating those same issues through entertainment venues, as witnessed by the growing number of television shows and motion pictures released over the last few years that deal with gay and lesbian characters and social concerns. Several come to mind: *Roseanne, Murphy Brown*, PBS's *Tales of the City*, films like *Philadelphia; Wigstock; Jeffrey; Priscilla, Queen of the Desert;* and *Priest.*

Heterosexual Americans may be bored with equal rights for lesbians and gay men, but they are fascinated with gay and lesbian lives. Greg Louganis's *Breaking the Surface* jumped to number one

▼ ▼ ▼ ▼ ▼ ▼ ▼ ▼ ▼ ▼ ▼ ▼ ▼ ▼ ▼ ▼ ▼ ▼ ▼ ▼

on the *New York Times* bestseller list in less than three weeks of its release. We couldn't get enough of the scandal surrounding Michael Jackson's alleged sleeping arrangements with young boys. And the afternoon talk shows continue to mesmerize us with every variation on gaydom imaginable. A mere decade ago, gay and lesbian visibility was largely segregated to a select few urban zip codes known as gay ghettos.

Those days are over. And so are the days of censoring gay and lesbian consumers in media, commercial advertising, and national entertainment venues. Although slow to occur legally, trends in the business realm are clearly moving toward sexual diversity, segmentation, targeting, and seeking out important new kinds of consumers with modern, innovative kinds of advertising.

Which brings us to the corporate dilemma of making room for effective gay and lesbian marketing strategies. Something that does not have to be as hard as it sounds.

Communicating Sensitivity

Marketing any consumer product today is tough. Just getting slightly ahead or making a product perform enough to maintain its market share requires brilliant writers and art directors, hyper-informed, shrewd-thinking account people, and ultrasophisticated, multilevel advertising campaigns.

Account people complain about the fine line they have to walk between making their clients feel comfortable with their creative team's work and the superiors they report to versus what is actually needed to deliver the numbers that will register as increased sales when the agency's contract comes up for review. Advertising creatives talk about the insanity, the pressure, and often the deviousness with which a product's quality is touted, misrepresented, or occasionally outright lied about as it is shoved into the limelight of mass consumption with flyer miles, rewards, rebates, replays, and customer loyalty programs. Anything will be tried to sell a product, push an agenda, communicate an idea, disenfranchise an institution, defame a competitor, or win an election.

Media people know that America is now a commercialized Orwellian jungle, that all ideals, programs, products, and images have to step into the same line of fire for a chance at the center

▼ ▼

stage in the amphitheater of mass consumerism. In television news, content is now secondary to the sensationalized visual imagery and the packaging of shock value—which is why news is no longer news but a product produced and spun by "media companies," all of which—including major newspapers—are now owned by one of twenty-three multinational corporations.[4]

Today, hype and controversy have become more than a deviation from a perceived norm: they have become the norm itself. And a visual norm, at that.

We don't read; we watch. We don't think; we choose from a list of options. Because our new, mega mass culture demands it. This new common denominator of controversy, this par of what I call the era of "managed-care shock value," applies not only to news and advertising now, but to nearly every aspect of daily life—including the very fabric of the democratic process itself. With the heightened emphasis on gay and lesbian market segments, it makes a company's advertising work even tougher, no matter whom it has a history of selling its product to. In many urban areas of the United States, sensitivity regarding advertising should be especially scrutinized by marketers, particularly when positioning products to lesbians of the baby boom generation who will respond much less to—or even reject—overly sexualized imagery. *Advocate* associate publisher Stephanie Blackwood agrees, stating that marketers should bear in mind that "lesbians in America [have been] conditioned based on twenty-five years of the women's movement."

What marketers need to understand is that gay and lesbian consumers are among the most sensitive of all American consumers when it comes to the potential dangers and implications of our overly commmercialized modern society.

They are especially aware of this because it is a society that has largely excluded them, forcing them to constantly reevaluate themselves and their relationships to the images at hand. Gay and lesbian consumers may not always be able to articulate these feelings, but they know it intuitively and indicate such perceptions in focus groups, to private therapists and social workers, and in national polls.

To communicate with gay and lesbian consumers is to reinvent sensitivity—to reengineer "realness" by communicating and mirroring the best in gay and lesbian culture as it is and "can be"—not as it has been assumed and stereotyped.

▼ ▼

The Slow Influence of the Gay Male Aesthetic

Until the late 1970s, the route regarding sensationalism and controversy in the use of sex to sell a product stopped abruptly at a problematic fork in the road: to the left was the depiction of same-sex affection beyond the platonic. This was a basic no-no—especially in the depiction of men's needs and desires. Women were allowed to be seen holding, touching, hugging and even adoring each other, because the rules of heterosexual behavior (in a male-dominated world) have always decreed such behavior as the rightful domain of being "feminine," being "passive," being ladylike. Any image that could be argued to be too "homosexually suggestive" (of men or women) was quietly accepted to be the road "safely not taken."

However, to the right of the fork in the road was endless closetry and lots of advertising code, particularly the increasing erotification of the male body—something that was just never done before, but continues to grow today, and comes directly out of urban gay male culture, politics, and its own self-informed sense of aesthetic constructionism. With regard to men and the domain of the masculine, subtly hinting at bisexuality was quietly permissible so long as there was a level of deniability in the creative execution—usually the token placement of a single woman.

Taking the right fork usually meant the the woman's body was the body that was eroticized. Men generally did not appear in advertising, on television, or in film, in any aggressively focused way that accentuated their bodies. That was the domain of the female flesh. Men appeared in bathing suits or with their shirts off in a love scene, that was about it. Men were sexualized by whether or not they had that distinguished touch of gray in their hair, if they had money, if they were youthful, gentlemanly, or great business-men. Men were sexual if they were single, they were sexy if they were married, but they were never objectified as sexual objects they way women were.

Much has changed.

Today there is so much mixed messaging and outright eroticizing of both sexes in any number of combinations that the proverbial fork in the marketing road has been nearly eliminated. There's very little line left to cross when it comes to sexuality, only varying degrees of creative boundary based on industry progressiveness,

▼ ▼

media buying, and perceived visual tolerances in relation to geography and demographics. The erotification of the male body is now as much required in the selling of products as is the accentuation of the female breast. And with all this new sexual permissiveness is finally coming a sense of sanity and experimentation toward the profitable new world of gay and lesbian marketing.

With each passing month, more and more companies are willing to explore and more realistically depict the heretofore forbidden realm of male and female romantic, same-sex affectionate behavior in mass advertising. It's most apparent in their modern treatment and erotification of the male form—something that has actually helped liberate heterosexual men. Today advertisers are beginning to get familiar with testing and launching advertising campaigns with intentionally identifiable gay and lesbian subject matter with increasing degrees of verisimilitude.

In New York City, a Hugo Boss advertising campaign on public transit buses shows three guys. Two are standing close to each other with one looking over his shoulder to the third, who is standing alone. The gentleman who is standing alone seems to be reacting to the two standing together. Is he supposed to be jealous? Perplexed? Wondering about the relationship of the two men standing together? Or is he supposed to be the guy "all alone" who needs to buy Hugo Boss to be a part of some particular group? Any combination of responses is possible depending on the perspective of the consumer.

Ambiguous and somewhat coded? Yes.

Progressive advertising? Certainly. Because it requires men, gay or straight, to ponder the image's intended messaging. The result is still the same: Hugo Boss on the brain of male consumers regardless of sexual orientation.

Sensitive and informed fashion, media, and advertising professionals understand these relationships—and have most recently used them to increase the visibility of lesbians.

But what is most interesting is the fact that the hottest visual product being sold to the American public in the nineties is not really the suggestion of gay and lesbian sexuality, or even affections, but a kind of pansexual understanding and sensitivity about multicultural unity. Calvin Klein's new cologne called One is a perfect example of this blurring new direction.

▼ ▼

The Explosive Emergence of the Modern Gay and Lesbian Consumer

Great events are happening where gay and lesbian consumers make purchasing decisions. They are also happening where they earn their living.

Through the systematic rewriting of equal opportunity employment policy statements in thousands of companies nationwide, gays and lesbians are effecting change on a profoundly fundamental level in American society. Insurance policies and employee benefit packages at major corporations are being rewritten, affecting the ability of corporations to attract and keep America's most educated, talented, and productive workers—both gay and straight.

It should not strike anyone as ironic that some of America's most progressive companies with the best track records on gay and lesbian workplace issues are also some of the most up-and-coming forces in the marketing of their industries' products to gay and lesbian consumers.

For the readers who are new to American gay and lesbian culture, in the equal rights movement for gay and lesbian citizens, or its relationship to the American economy, three strategic points need to be understood: 1) media has misrepresented the character and demographics of American gay and lesbian culture; 2) Americans of homosexual orientation feel all the same emotions about life, God, and country as Americans of heterosexual orientation; and 3) gay and lesbian culture in the Western world has undergone more cataclysmic change in the past fifteen years than at any time in recorded history.

All the varying social issues and economic challenges that are faced daily by heterosexual Americans—whether as citizens, parents, consumers, teenagers, veterans, or employees—also exist in varying degrees for lesbians and gay men in every city, town, and rural community in America.

All the phobias, ignorance, and tensions relating to race, religion, status, income, class, and education also apply in varying degrees to the lives of gays and lesbians—including the historical compulsion to render women of all backgrounds essentially invisible.[5]

While gay and lesbian visibility is higher today than it has ever been in the modern world, it must be readily accepted as fact that

▼ ▼

vast numbers of bisexuals, lesbians, and gay men have always worked in the American economy since the founding of the republic—indeed in the history of humankind.

Recognizing oneself as gay, lesbian, or bisexual is an orientational, emotional, physical, political, (and now) economic "identity" in exactly the visceral way that being straight is an "identity." One is one's sexuality; something that is a complex conglomeration of an individual's personal and spiritual essence.

The politics and understanding of identity and its relationship to freedom and expression in media is constantly evolving. Consider the following passage:

> Homosexuals are discarding their furtive ways and openly admitting, even flaunting, their deviation. Homosexuals have their own drinking places, their special assignation streets, even their own organizations. And for every obvious homosexual, there are probably nine nearly impossible to detect. This social disorder, which society tries to suppress, has forced itself into the public eye because it does present a problem—and parents especially are concerned.

This was the lead paragraph in a *Life* magazine article just thirty years ago. When this passage is compared to the Nut and Honey cereal commercials, one can see how it might be construed by some that things really changed very little in marketing between the early 1960s and the late 1980s.

All through those years the sea of perpetuated myths transmitted to heterosexual Americans said that gays and lesbians were immoral and criminal by repeatedly using the word *deviant* or psychologically sick by characterizing them as being prissy degenerates at the root of a "social disorder." And nearly all references refused to acknowledge that women could also be gay, because that was an equally radical notion, which would have required that the word *lesbian* be printed in a national publication.

A second article on the psychology of homosexuality in the same issue of *Life* stated that "a bad case of acne, a stammer or unusual shyness may make a boy feel so unwanted in the world of boy-meets-girl that he quickly embraces the other world." The article included a parenthetical aside stating that "many a homosexual affair . . . is an alliance between two men who both consider themselves 'social cripples.'"[6]

▼ ▼

It was against this historical perspective of gay and lesbian Americans in the mainstream media that gay and lesbian individuals started their own newspapers, their own political groups, and, essentially, their own culture. By 1975, the national gay and lesbian community was galloping full steam ahead toward becoming an important new marketplace.

The beginning of this phenomenon was certainly elusive, but it was solid—so solid, in fact, that motion picture producers, liquor distributors, boutiques, and theatrical performance revues were beginning to discreetly advertise to gays and lesbians. Word of this evolution began to tease the mainstream. It was calmly documented in the *Wall Street Journal* as early as 1975.[7]

Yet outside of some brief mentions in trade articles (and an infuriating but motivating rallying call to gay activism inadvertently provided by Anita Bryant) few noticed that gay and lesbian culture was becoming more than a political movement. Few would have even believed that it was in fact on its way to becoming one of the most important economic and cultural forces the twentieth century would see.

But many gays and lesbians saw and felt the changes everywhere. And much of the country danced right alongside them not realizing that a new consumer revolution was gearing up. Gloria Gaynor belted it out loud and clear and made it stick: "Never Can Say Good-bye," which stayed on the Billboard Top 40 for ten weeks. All of America simply "danced to the beat of the disco" and the sound of the Village People's rallying tribal-call song, "Macho Man," which bolted out of radios ad nauseum.

Gay and lesbian culture was simply beginning to enchant the mainstream marketplace. It was evident in the way gay-inspired writers influenced Bette Midler and her cult following of gays and lesbians (and eventually Middle America, with the help of Walt Disney Studios). It was evident in the following that the Pointer Sisters were developing. Rock music stars like David Bowie and the Rolling Stones dripped with androgyny. And Janis Ian, Rock Hudson, Paul Lynn, the British music invasion, Levi's button-fly jeans, earrings for men, the women's music movement—all had subtle gay overtones that woke up gay men and lesbians (and some product marketers) throughout the country even though much of heterosexual America didn't notice any of it as being a "gay influence."

But that was before anyone had been diagnosed.

▼ ▼

Communicating Legitimacy in an Age of Grief

By the early 1980s, the AIDS epidemic had crystallized and magnified nearly every issue that gay and lesbian citizens had been confronting throughout American history.

AIDS, in effect, mainstreamed gay and lesbian visibility in the United States. It exponentially increased gay and lesbian political coverage in media at both national and local levels. In time, the media became more levelheaded in its coverage of gays and lesbians, but with the increased visibility came a near proportional increase in violence against gays and lesbians nationwide.

A domino effect began.

Political rhetoric heated up on Capitol Hill and in state legislatures across the country. Religious groups began trumping up the crackpot medical lies of the nineteenth century, using the power of the religious broadcasting networks to disseminate falsehoods and politically self-serving information about morality, the wrath of God, and the breakdown of the family (something that went on in the nineteenth century as well).

Radical health officials began arguing for quarantines; political extremists called for tattooing of people testing HIV positive.

For the American gay and lesbian community, being "out" and being visible became literally tantamount to staying alive.

Many gay and lesbian citizens became terrified, even fearful that the country was drifting toward fascism. Indeed, it appeared to them that a precedent of silence was about to return from the McCarthy era—particularly since Ronald Reagan looked (and turned out to be) no more a friend to gay men and lesbians than Eisenhower turned out to be in 1950s.

It was under these conditions that gay and lesbian activism, visibility, and consumerism erupted with a vengeance unseen since Stonewall.

We watched CNN as ACT-UP demonstrators disrupted business at the New York Stock Exchange in an attempt to wake people up about the hypocrisy in the health care industry and how big business was price-gouging the dying.

We watched AIDS activists march into St. Patrick's Cathedral in New York City disrupting Mass and demanding to know why American taxpayer money was going to hospitals run by the Catholic Church—an institution that refuses to acknowledge the importance

▼ ▼

of educating people about condom use to prevent the spread of HIV.

A courageous new gay and lesbian magazine called *Outweek* was thrust onto national newsstands. It dared to call Madison Avenue's bluff by removing all its sexually oriented advertising and then reminded wholesalers across the country that they would be in violation of restraint of trade legislation if they refused to place the publication in suburban retail outlets.

Outweek printed the same kind of intimate journalism about people's lives that Ann Landers counseled on, Liz Smith gossiped about, and Rona Barrett tattled on about heterosexuals for years. It also printed the truth about Covenant House in New York City and Malcom Forbes's attraction to young men, and it exposed the carefully hidden secrets behind Washington's and Hollywood's hypocrisy, lies, and double standards.

None of these developments served to make the business world comfortable with advertising to gay and lesbian consumers. Consequently, for a few years it didn't really matter how much statistical information was being presented by gay and lesbian political leaders, market authorities, and newspaper publishers—corporations were not ready to jump into the gay and lesbian marketplace because it looked to be a sure public relations fiasco.

In retrospect, however, *Outweek* and other groups' amplification of gay, lesbian, and AIDS activism magnanimously prompted a much-needed nationwide shift in thinking. Suddenly new financial contributions began flowing into the nation's AIDS organizations from once closeted public figures. New films and television programs came out of Hollywood with more accurate portrayals of gay and lesbian people; AIDS and human rights concerns began caressing night-time television dramas.

More domestic partnership task forces cropped up at large corporations and small businesses around the country, allowing more gay and lesbian employees to petition for the same spousal benefits that their heterosexual co-workers enjoyed. The 1990s saw more celebrities, actors, musicians, and politicians coming out publicly as gays and lesbians, activists, and modern revolutionaries in true Jeffersonian style than in all the decades of the twentieth century put together.

Finally, in concert with America's telecommunications explosion, the ever-present thirst for a sound bite, and a new twist on the old, the country woke up from its traditional perspective about human sexual-

▼ ▼

ity: It had stumbled upon gay and lesbian Americans because there was an increase in the amount of coverage on the issues that concerned them.

Ironically, with all the verbal gay-bashing that occurred at the Republican National Convention in Houston, Texas, many issues of concern to gay, lesbian, and bisexual Americans were moved all the more rapidly to the forward serving sections of America's commercial steam table.

In the mid 1980s, AIDS indirectly brought more attention to lesbian mothers, gay male fathers, and the transgendered community—all of which became the mainstay of great afternoon talk show subjects because they simply up the ante on sexual voyeurism in the media. Gay subject matter developed into a consistent and dynamic theme in television entertainment, doing for afternoon ratings what violence apparently can do for evening ratings.

But over time those subjects became commonplace discussion. By the 1990s, the talk shows were beginning to explore outing, gay and lesbian palimony, discrimination in the armed services, the sinister corporate behavior of the insurance industry, and the constrictions it was placing on gay and lesbian families.

Against all the cable television competition and hype, there was a consistent baptizing of public consciousness about real gay and lesbian Americans—that they do suffer abuse by their government, lose their jobs, their children, their health insurance—in fact, their very lives. Hype had given way to a degree of reality.

On a scale unprecedented heterosexual American society began experiencing and understanding through media for the first time what gays and lesbians, as a group, experienced in the Harlem Renaissance and the flourishing of Bohemia early in the century: a more collective and mirrored self-awareness of the nation's diverse sexual makeup. The growth and legitimacy of gay and lesbian culture in America had at long last become utterly unavoidable. Newsrooms couldn't deny the size of the marches that were growing around the country.

The Gay and Lesbian Alliance Against Defamation formed chapters in every major city. Queer Nation was born. The Lesbian Avengers came into being. Both got press.

The public became astonished (but was later enchanted) by the sheer inclusiveness and friendliness of gay and lesbian freedom day parades and the shrewd effectiveness and ability of activists to cap-

▼ ▼

ture international television coverage and raise public consciousness on a number of issues—almost on a daily basis. The AIDS crisis
further forced the country to acknowledge the extent to which gay
and lesbian culture existed, and that tens of thousands of gays and
lesbians (and heterosexuals) were now dying of an epidemic.

Today there is a new era of candidness about gay and lesbian culture in America. It is a candidness that is allowing business to begin
listening to the logic of America's gay and lesbian newspaper publishers, advertising sales executives, direct marketers, and event
coordinators.

In midsize American cities, the increase of visibility of gays and
lesbians has likewise become directly proportional to the degree of
intolerance being displayed by local area politicians—especially
when the intolerance is more representative of political strategy at
the expense of gays and lesbians, rather than of voting con-
stituency.

This dynamic, for instance, was recently apparent in Indianapolis,
when the state legislature temporarily decided against including the
words *sexual orientation* in an intensely debated hate crimes bill. At
the time, the legislature refused to protect its gay and lesbian citizens
(claiming it would be legitimizing a "lifestyle"). This social bigotry
brought out more gay and lesbian activists across Indiana than ever
before, fueling a debate over sexual politics unlike any Indiana had
ever seen. Gay and lesbian issues began filling the radio airwaves and
nightly newscasts of Indiana's television screens. The *Indianapolis Star
and News* began regularly assessing sexual politics on its editorial
page, placing a variety of issues surrounding gay and lesbian emancipation, civil rights, and individual liberty protections on the front
burner of Indiana politics.

For the first time, gay and lesbian Hoosiers were prime-time news.
A media item. A new local area commodity sandwiched between
General Motors car commercials, Pacers basketball scores, and agri-
cultural farming reports.

But it didn't stop there. Gay and lesbian issues were being discussed in the workplace with a greater degree of intensity. Gay and
lesbian Hoosiers began rereading their employee benefits manuals
at work, looking for the words *sexual orientation* in their companies'
hiring and employment practices.

And when gay and lesbian freedom month came around in June,
more people attended their local area celebration than ever before

in the state's history. And it was not just gay men and lesbians in attendance; they brought their children, their friends, and their parents—most of whom will now be more discriminating in their purchase of products and placing of votes during elections.

That event alone (Indiana's public gay and lesbian celebrations had begun only four years earlier) required street vending permits for over forty businesses hoping to attract gay and lesbian consumers. Most of all, it set a pioneering, visible precedent of free enterprise and gay and lesbian respect for individual rights in the middle of America's heartland for years to come.

Consequently, all across the country politics is showing just how responsive both business and gay and lesbian consumers, their families, and friends can be in cities as conservative as Indianapolis when it comes to individual rights. It shows that, in cities large and small, market dynamics are tied to increasing levels of tolerance of gay and lesbian visibility and respect for individuality for all Americans.

In New York City, for example, the higher level of tolerance toward gays and lesbians directly affected the turnout for the 25th anniversary of the Stonewall Riots, which coincided with the Gay Games IV and Cultural Festival. City comptroller Alan Hevisi conservatively estimated that the 1994 Gay Games IV celebration brought in well over $400 million to the New York City economy. And that is not counting the hundreds of thousands of dollars racked up at airlines and travel agencies from around the world.

At that same time, AT&T launched its first gay and lesbian direct-marketing campaign aimed specifically at tens of thousands of known gay and lesbian households in all fifty states, implicitly expressing their support for the importance of gay and lesbian political issues and simultaneously urging them to switch their long-distance service to AT&T.

That same month Perrier and Calistoga bottled water began running advertisements in gay and lesbian papers and magazines across the United States. Miller Beer joined with AT&T and Continental Airlines in sponsoring the Gay Games, which crescendoed before a sellout crowd in Yankee Stadium with a performance by Patti Labelle and, the following day, in a march ending in Central Park with a concert performance by Liza Minnelli.

Clearly, gay and lesbian pride celebrations each June create a steady and important rhythm around which gay activists, gay con-

▼ ▼

sumers, and gay-friendly companies can rally. They also serve to keep a sense of visibility and civic responsibility instilled in younger gay and lesbian groups as the national media slowly relearns how to interpret and report gay and lesbian news in its proper context, without being afraid to be critical or overly bias in its observations.

Business has come to understand that gay and lesbian con-sumerism is not a flash in the pan but an evolving and stable, long-term development in modern marketing.

What business must now accept is that the media has ironically fallen prey to its own infatuation with the gay market story—which has resulted in more misrepresentation and harsh statistical stereotyping about gay and lesbian affluence. This mischaracteri-zation of facts has been further fueled by overzealousness on behalf of some gay-owned research firms and publishers that have sought to portray out-of-context research and demographic infor-mation about gay and lesbian magazine readers as being repre-sentative of the gay and lesbian population nationwide. This has led to the development of more myths about gay and lesbian Americans—that they supposedly all live in dual income earning households with no children and a higher than average dispos-able income allowing them to take worldwide vacations and drink premium scotch whiskies while listening to Vivaldi. Which, of course, is not true.

What is true is that a favorable portion of some dual-earning, urban gay male, baby-boomer households do appear to have an above average disposable income. But the fiction loitering around most television and newspaper newsrooms about the vast majority of gay and lesbian Americans and their money is simply misguided, sloppily researched, and improperly characterized.

The American media's ongoing carelessness in reporting gay and lesbian economic news has lead to an inexcusable level of misinfor-mation being picked up and used by right-wing extremists as an argument to roll back gay and lesbian equal rights gains at many municipal levels (as if affluence were a reason to deny an American his or her rights).

Unfortunately for marketers, much of the economic research prior to 1993 surrounding income and parenthood among the majority of gays and lesbians is not useful in understanding them as a national group. According to the independent research conducted exclusively for this book by the world-renowned con-

▼ ▼

sumer research firm, Yankelovich Partners, much previous research appears to be astonishingly inaccurate or based on methods that no industry trade publication would dare use to explain anything about heterosexual consumers. Which is why, in the next chapter, we will place a big gay/lesbian magnifying glass on all the studies worth looking at, what they say, and what they don't. And how business can make better, more useful sense of it all.

▼ ▼

WHO IS THE GAY AND LESBIAN AMERICAN CONSUMER?

The social values of human activities must be measured by many scales other than those which are available to the scientist.

DR. ALFRED KINSEY[1]

Have you ever heard of the lucrative heterosexual market? Probably not.

A heterosexual market, per se, has never really existed in marketing language. But until recently nearly all consumer marketing was nothing but heterosexual. It was built around growth of the nuclear family, housing starts, savings for the kid's college tuition, etc.

It wasn't until the visibility and growth of the gay and lesbian political, cultural, and consumer revolution came about that any other kind of consumer buying pattern besides those based on heterosexuality was even considered by marketers. Even as segmentation became more the norm, we really began aiming our marketing toward "segments of heterosexuals"—consumers we could identify in more focused ways, but ways that were taken for granted as being straight, not gay or lesbian.

Today, leading companies are applying the science of segmentation in a way that includes gay and lesbian consumers as well as heterosexual consumers. But a marketer's understanding and the strategies he or she employs in the pursuit of gay and lesbian consumers must be applied in the same, segmented ways that have been applied in the marketing of products to heterosexuals. Gay

▼ ▼

and lesbian market "segments" exist in much the same way that heterosexual market "segments" exist. And determining the size and breakdown of each of those gay and lesbian segments requires the same kind of approach that has been used to determine the demographics, human values, needs, wants, fears, and dreams in the segments of what were once assumed to be all straight consumers.

So, in determining the demographics and psychographics of the modern consumer marketplace, our focus needs to begin including sexual identity as part of the overall marketing strategy. And our focus on gay and lesbian consumers, per se, must be of a segmented, targetable nature as well.

Soon, indeed very soon, all consumer market segmentation analysis will have to take into account the degree to which product and service sales are made up of gay and lesbian buying patterns if companies want to keep the gay and lesbian consumers they have, or want to attract new gay and lesbian consumers in the future.

Elevating the Discussion and the Science

Without digressing into the politics of identity, let alone the academic arguments surrounding constructionist versus essentialist views of human sexuality, it is important to remember that any number sighted as a measure of a gay or lesbian population in the United States is only as good as the methodology used to arrive at it.

To begin to quantify the potential gay and lesbian marketplace, I have compiled quick overviews of all the relevant studies pertaining in some way to gay and lesbian consumerism that were conducted in this century. Most of the studies have sought to understand gay and lesbian sexuality and how that sexuality exists within the larger heterosexual majority. However, some do shed interesting light on economics.

But first, some basic questions must be addressed regarding how these studies were conducted and what they say or don't say about gay and lesbian consumers in America.

Was convenience or random sampling used to obtain the participants? Are the results generalizable or scientifically applicable to the population as a whole, and therefore representative and logically supportive of the conclusions drawn? Were questionnaires, interviews, and observations conducted face-to-face? Were written

▼ ▼

documents and questionnaires presented in a confidential setting or an anonymous setting? (There is a difference.)

Recently more and more studies have been cited as the latest source for determining the number of gay men and lesbians in the United States. Upon closer scrutiny, however, most of the studies cited merely investigated varying degrees of sexual behavior in the human species—the studies did not conclude that the individual saw him- or herself as "being" gay or lesbian. Nor did those studies arrive at conclusions based on that behavior that would help marketers consider such individuals as prospective customers in a targeted "gay-or-lesbian-oriented" advertising campaign.

Researching and analyzing sexual behavior, sexual orientation, and how these impact on an individual's sense of sexual identity is tough work. It all requires highly sophisticated methodology, competent scientists, rock-solid funding, and political proficiency in academic circles.

When we apply these dynamics to the science of consumer behavior, and then attempt to understand their relationships to our increasingly segmented and globally interactive marketplace, we are faced with a number of complex problems that appear insurmountable. A mere study of sexual behavior will not answer the questions today's businesspeople want answered about gay and lesbian people as consumers.

All of these problems, however, do not mean that economists, psychologists, political pollsters, and market researchers are incapable of coming up with a reasonably acceptable estimate of the likely size of the self-identified American gay and lesbian population. Or that researchers can't determine how varying groups of gay and lesbian consumers think, shop, save, and spend their money differently from heterosexual consumers.

Such numbers and meaningful, more reliable data do exist, and depending on who you listen to and hold accountable, they indeed have significant relevance to understanding the art and science of gay and lesbian consumer economics. But a delineation between studies and what they actually represent must be addressed.

Which takes us to the Yankelovich MONITOR® Gay and Lesbian Perspective—the most important research conducted on gay and lesbian consumers to date.

The Yankelovich MONITOR research on gay and lesbian Americans is unlike any other study in the United States because it seeks to

▼ ▼

understand gay and lesbian consumer thinking and behavior, as opposed to sexual behavior and conditioning. This research addresses, much more accurately and comprehensively, the questions business wants answered about gay and lesbian demographics and psychographics in relation to the economics of the population as a whole, based on random sampling and weighted against U.S. Census data.

Before briefly summarizing the various studies and then making my case for some general conclusions in relation to Yankelovich MONITOR findings, here are a couple of reminders regarding the basics of sexually oriented research, and how the media's somewhat casual use of sexually oriented language has diluted the public's understanding of the facts. The first regards sex, and the second regards identity and who we are talking about when we say "the gay and lesbian marketplace."

Plenty of studies have attempted to determine the number of people, by sex, in the human species who have ever had a homosexual experience. But such studies are of relatively little use in determining the number of American consumers who see themselves as gay or lesbian—and are therefore likely to respond to the commercial environment in a way that is of interest to marketers.

Businesspeople must accept that the American gay and lesbian economy is a growing and vast panorama of distinctly targetable market segments made up of diverse groups of citizens whose racial, sexual, religious, political, and economic identity is, in varying degrees, informed by their sexual orientation—but also by their individual life experience.

The number of targetable gay and lesbian market segments, and the total sum of prospective gay and lesbian consumers that number represents, is not at all equal to some scientific estimate of the number of people in the human species who have ever had a romantic or sexual experience with a member of the same sex.

Simply put: The incidence of homosexual behavior in the population is not proportional to the number of gay and lesbian consumers that can be targeted by a company, political party, or marketing study group. For marketers, it really does not matter how many people are having, are likely to have, or have at some time had, a sexual experience with a member of the same sex. Sexual behavior alone is not a barometer of whether or not an individual can be considered part of any prospective consumer cohort.

Still, a marketer must obviously be able to determine where

the prospective customers are. Therefore, what really matters is being able to determine the total number of individuals who "self-identify" as being gay or lesbian within any given geographic area. However, they must be given a scientifically fair and equal opportunity to do so.

The concept of *self-identity* remains as the most important dynamic that must be addressed and considered before relying on any data claiming to represent the size of gay and lesbian consumer populations anywhere. If we can't at least determine who is identifiable, then how can we determine who to target?

Reading Between the Lines

Now a quick word about shortcomings in sexual research. The most common involve the manner in which individuals are obtained for the research—including the way in which they are questioned.

Many sexually oriented studies arrive at conclusions based on "convenience sampling," meaning that participants are obtained through institutions, government offices, schools, public health clinics. In some cases they are approached in shopping malls, public events, and transportation terminals and then paid to participate. Kinsey's research has been cited for this particular shortcoming because some of his critics believed that too many of his participants came from medical institutions, prisons, and schools and therefore gave a biased view of sexuality (particularly with regards to homosexuality in men). When convenience samples are used in sexually oriented research, the probability that the conclusions will be projectable to the national population becomes highly questionable.

The most reliable research—in terms of projectability to the overall population—needs to be based on what is often referred to as "random probability," meaning that participants in the survey have been selected in a scientifically hygienic way, insuring that their responses will be reasonably representative of the general population with regard to geography, race, ethnicity, religion, education, culture bias, etc. The Yankelovich MONITOR Gay and Lesbian Perspective meets this rigid requirement.[2]

How We Got to Where We Are

During the 1980s, many advertising-starved gay and lesbian publications across the United States set out to identify, study, and publish

▼ ▼

information highlighting their readers' income, affluence, and education.

Since newspaper and magazine readers (in fact, readers in general) tend to be more educated and have a higher disposable income than those individuals who don't subscribe to periodicals, a new stereotype began brewing about the wealth of gay Americans. This notion came about largely because the statistics that were getting media coverage were based on biased information—that of newspaper readerships opposed to scientifically researched income levels generalized to the self-identified gay and lesbian population.

In actuality, the majority of lesbians and gay men in the United States earn slightly less than heterosexuals. This fact was demonstrated in a recent study conducted by economist Lee Badgett of the University of Maryland.[3] Ms. Badgett's recent findings parallel research conducted by Yankelovich Partners, which also found that self-identified gay and lesbian Americans do not earn more than heterosexuals.

1994 Yankelovich MONITOR Gay/Lesbian Perspective

	Gay/Lesbian %	Heterosexual %
PERSONAL INCOME:		
Under $25K	85	78
$25K–$49,999	12	19
$50K–$99,999	2	3
$100K+	1	*
HOUSEHOLD INCOME:		
Under $25K	44	38
$25K–$49,999	39	39
$50K–$99,999	14	20
$100K+	3	3
MEAN PERSONAL INCOME (000)	**$16.9**	**$17.6**
MEAN HOUSEHOLD INCOME (000)	**$35.8**	**$36.7**
MEAN HOUSEHOLD SIZE	**2.89**	**3.01**

*Less than 0.5%

▼ ▼

The wealthiest proportion of gay and lesbian Americans that exists is segregated to a minority of older, dual-income, white male *households* in the country's largest urban areas, which represents only a fraction of the entire self-identified gay and lesbian population size. Since men tend to earn more than women, it is only natural that this all-male minority would have a higher household income than one comprised of a man and a lower-earning woman.

Still, the idea that gay and lesbian Americans are more affluent is the impression that most Americans were left with after the media explosion discovered gay and lesbian consumerism, but focused on the gay—meaning male part of the story—most predominantly. To a certain extent, the misconception awakened many in business to the nature of gay and lesbian market segments—even though the shattering of the myth of more widespread affluence was somewhat of a letdown in the short term for early pioneering marketers.

Still, the end result has been that nobody in marketing is disputing the fact any longer that gay and lesbian consumers are everywhere. Especially after the hundreds of thousands of people made their identities very clear by participating in the 1993 gay and lesbian national march on Washington and the 1994 Gay Games IV and 25th anniversary of the Stonewall Riots in New York City.

Identifying the Consumers That Matter

In a mid-size American city of say two million residents, the difference between a study that claims 10 percent of population to be gay or lesbian (200,000 people) versus 2 percent (40,000) is basically irrelevant in discussions about an individual's rights.

Individual rights are individual rights whether they're applied to 2 million, 200,000, 40,000, or 4. In a marketing context, however, numbers and methodology become very relevant: 40,000 potential consumers in any combination of segments in a given geographic region is significantly different than 200,000.

Until the complete presentation of the Yankelovich MONITOR's Gay and Lesbian Perspective was made available in this book, no widely published study in the history of market research has representatively examined the behavior and number of individuals in the United States who identify as being gay, lesbian, or homosexual within the context of consumer activity and thinking.

No doubt some parallels may be found between existing research on sexual behavior of gays and lesbians and consumer behavior of

▼ ▼

the population as a whole, but these parallels are insufficient in determining the more sophisticated issues directly pertaining to identity and gay and lesbian psychographics.

According to John Knoebel, vice president of *The Advocate,* some preliminary research was conducted by the Walker Struman research firm in 1968. This ground-breaking study of the readership of *The Advocate,* then one of the few gay and lesbian publications in the United States (at the time readership was almost exclusively male; the word *lesbian* did not appear on the cover of *The Advocate* until 1990), was probably the first professional study of gay and lesbian consumers.

The late Frank Vinci, former advertising director for *The Advocate,* recalls the demand for Walker Struman's research and even remembers "other [publishing] companies stealing the information" and using it to sell the affluence and education of *The Advocate*'s gay and lesbian market to their potential advertisers.

Other than *The Advocate*'s early research, none of the previous studies of homosexuality conducted in this century were motivated by the need for consumer behavioral information; they were largely commissioned out of a need to know about sexual behavior exclusively or the degree to which such status should be interpreted and recognized in the evaluation of policy (as in the case of the Rand report on sexual orientation and U.S. military personnel policy).

As a general rule, research indicates that the larger population

	Total Population %	Gay/Lesbian %
METROPOLITAN AREA SIZE:		
3 million+	19	27
1–3 million	27	34
500K–999,999	13	12
250K–499,999	10	8
100K–249,999	9	5
Non-Met Area	22	14
	100	100
ALL COUNTIES IN 25 LARGEST METROS:	**39**	**56**

▼ ▼

centers of the country are where the most self-identified gay and lesbian consumers are to be found. The chart on the previous page shows how the percentages break down by population for those gay and lesbian individuals who identified themselves in the Yankelovich study.

Just looking at known gay and lesbian consumer markets based on population percentages is only a base point by which companies can begin targeting gay and lesbian consumers. In the long run, independently conducted research aimed at a company's current or developing gay and lesbian consumer base is the best way to develop a strategy for keeping those customers and learning how to go after the competition's gay and lesbian customers as well. In addition, marketers need to monitor and understand how their current gay and lesbian consumers are interacting in the local marketplace.

For instance, winter coats are not, of course, going to sell as briskly to gay and lesbian consumers in Southern California as they are in the northeastern part of the country. But a certain kind of coat by a particular manufacturer in New York, for instance, may do better with gay or lesbian consumers over another, say, imported brand. Obviously, only localized research in that region is going to shed light on such a question.

In addition, a point needs to be made regarding the visibility of well-populated areas of self-identified gay and lesbian consumers. Some might appear to be lacking a well-organized gay and lesbian political community, but that does not necessarily mean there is a lack of gay and lesbian consumer prospects. Sometimes the most quiet of gay and lesbian communities make the best sales prospects—this is especially worth considering when launching direct-mail campaigns.

For instance, some of the country's smaller cities and communities have heavily populated and active gay and lesbian consumer economies but comparatively tamer gay and lesbian activist groups and less nationally recognized levels of political visibility—particularly vacation areas such as Provincetown, Massachusetts; the Russian River area in Northern California; Austin, Texas; Hawaii; Ft. Lauderdale; Miami; and Key West, Florida. But all are excellent geographic areas worthy of target marketing campaigns and inclusion in multilevel print advertising buys when considering regional sales prospects.

▼ ▼

Population Estimates on Gay and Lesbian Americans

I have compiled the charts on the next page by extrapolating a sampling of various studies and their population estimates arrived at for the total number of gay Americans by race, religion, and geography in relation to the 1990 census report. These graphics illustrate in black and white just how divergent the range of conclusions is when gay or lesbian population percentages are compared side by side and in relation to the country as a whole.

I've started with the single most verifiable number—the 1990 census—and then compared it to the most liberal estimate (Kinsey 1948), to the most conservative (Guttmacher 1993), to the most representative of both sexes (Harris 1988 from the Rand Report), to the most representative average of self-identified gay men and lesbians (Yankelovich MONITOR 1994). For our purposes, the Yankelovich MONITOR conclusions are the most relevant in these charts because they represent self-identified individuals based on the study's findings *as a national average.* (To be more specific, the largest cities tend to have a geographic average closer to 9 percent and the rural areas more around 3 percent. See the chart in the next chapter for the exact percentage that should be applied to each city population based on the rate of self-identification.)

In addition to this sampling of population estimates, I've included a nuts and bolts review of all the studies that bear relevance to gay and lesbian marketplace issues.

The Defense Department Research, 1992

The report's official name was "Sexual Orientation and U.S. Military Personnel Policy: Options and Assessment National Defense Research Institute MR-323-OSD."[4] This highly publicized study did not include any laboratory or field research on homosexuality of its own. It analyzed existing research that it chose using a stringent set of criteria based on a general sampling methodology and then drew conclusions based on an overall assessment of the chosen reports.

The Rand Report was sponsored by the Office of the Secretary of Defense under Rand's National Defense Research Institute, a federally funded research and development center supported by the

Range of U.S. Gay and Lesbian Population Estimates by Race

1990 Census[1] Race/%	Population[1]	10% Kinsey	3.6% Harris	1% Guttmacher	6% Yankelovich
White/80.3%	199,686,070	19,968,607	7,188,699	1,996,861	11,981,164
Black/12.1%	29,986,060	2,998,606	1,079,498	299,861	1,799,164
American Indian, Eskimo, or Aleut/0.8%	1,959,234	195,923	70,532	19,592	117,554
Asian or Pacific Islander/2.9%	7,273,662	727,366	261,852	72,737	436,420
Other/3.9%	9,804,847	980,485	352,974	98,048	588,291
Total	248,709,873	24,870,987	8,953,555	2,487,099	14,922,593
Hispanic origin/9.0%[2]	22,354,059	2,235,406	804,746	223,541	1,341,244

[1]Source: 1994 Information Please Almanac
[2]Persons of Hispanic origin can be of any race

Range of U.S. Gay and Lesbian Population Estimates by Religion

1990 Census[1] Religion/%	Population[1]	10% Kinsey	3.6% Harris	1% Guttmacher	6% Yankelovich
Protestant/61%	151,713,023	15,171,302	5,461,669	1,517,130	9,102,781
Roman Catholic/25%	62,177,468	6,217,747	2,238,389	621,775	3,730,648
Jewish/2%	4,974,197	497,420	179,071	49,742	298,452
Other/5%	12,435,494	1,234,549	447,678	124,355	746,130
None/7%	17,409,691	1,740,969	626,749	174,097	1,044,581
Total	248,709,873	24,870,987	8,953,555	2,487,099	14,922,592

[1]Source: 1994 Information Please Almanac

▼ ▼

Office of the Secretary of Defense (at the time Les Aspin) and the Joint Chiefs of Staff.

Five studies of sexuality were cited in the Rand Report, including sample characteristics, prevalence of same-gender sexual contact, methods of data collection, and response rates. The studies and research organizations cited are:

- The National Opinion Research Council
- The General Social Survey Study
- Louis Harris and Associates
- Research Triangle Institute
- National Survey of Men

The table on pages 60–61 illustrates the basic conclusions that these studies came to regarding "prevalence of same-gender sexual contact," which, as I've argued, is significantly different from individuals who self-identify as being gay or lesbian within a consumer research study.

The Kinsey Research, 1948

According to his close research associate, Wardell B. Pomeroy, "Kinsey's two landmark volumes, *Sexual Behavior in the Human Male* (1948) and *Sexual Behavior in the Human Female* (1953), raised one of the most violent and widespread storms since Darwin, not only in the scientific community but among the public at large."

Citing these two volumes, Pomeroy writes in *Dr. Kinsey and the Institute for Sex Research*, "It is fair to say that Kinsey brought sex out of the bedroom and into the world's parlor. If he did not succeed in making it completely respectable, he laid the foundation for the greater freedom of sexual behavior and the far better understanding of it that we have today."[5]

A portion of Dr. Kinsey's conclusion on homosexuality was that about 10 percent of the males in his study reported to have had same-gender sex exclusively within a given period of three years. However, only 4 percent claimed to have been exclusively homosexual for the majority of their adult lives. Dr. Kinsey also concluded that an incidence of homosexuality among females was roughly one-third to one-half that of men. He had intended to do more comprehensive studies on women but died in 1956 before the research was completed. The 10 percent figure commonly heard in

▼ ▼

relation to gay and lesbian population estimates is only applicable to men, at best, and is, for both sexes, highly uncorrelatable to the national population forty years later.

Still, Kinsey's qualitative and quantitative research on men has its strengths, and the conclusions he arrived at regarding population percentages should not be totally excluded when observing consumer markets in large urban areas. Although Kinsey's methodology utilized face-to-face interviews, which tend to diminish accurate responses about being exclusively homosexual, he did come up with relatively high percentages of homosexual conduct for the times—many of which mirror studies conducted in the past few years.

Dr. Kinsey's report had many strengths despite the fact that his convenience sampling method (obtaining too many participants that may be biased) did not meet the standards of the Rand Corporation for the U.S. Department of Defense study. Among them, it had an extremely large sample size (12,000 participants); extremely comprehensive questioning, covering an extraordinary minimum of 350 items and in some cases as many as 521. It is one of the single most comprehensive studies of male sexuality ever conducted in history.[6]

The impeccable standards that Dr. Kinsey employed in his testing techniques are best captured in the words of Wardell B. Pomeroy:

> We asked our questions directly without hesitancy or apology.
>
> Kinsey correctly pointed out that if we were uncertain or embarrassed in our questioning we could not expect to get anything but a corresponding response. Unlike previous researchers, we did not say "touching yourself" when we meant masturbation, or "relations with other persons" when sexual intercourse was intended. "Evasive terms invite dishonest answers," was Kinsey's dictum. We also never asked whether a subject had ever engaged in a particular activity; we assumed that everyone had engaged in everything, and so we began by asking when he had first done it. Thus the subject who might want to deny an experience had a heavier burden placed on him, and since he knew from the way the question was asked that it would not surprise us if he had done it, there seemed little reason to deny it. . . .
>
> We looked our subjects squarely in the eye and fired the questions at them as fast as we could. These were two of our best guarantees against falsifying our responses. . . . [7]

Estimates of Homosexual Behavior from U.S. Probability Studies

Study	Sample Characteristics	Prevalence of Same-Gender Sexual Contact		Methods of Data Collection	Response Rate
		MALE	FEMALE		
National Opinion Research Council (NORC) 1970 (Fay et al., 1989)	1,450 men aged 21 and older	Since age 20 6.7% Last year 1.6–2.0%	N/A N/A	SAQ following face-to-face interview	N/A
General Social Survey (GSS)[1] 1989–91	1,564 men and 1,963 women aged 18 and older 1,941 men and 2,163 women aged 18 and older	Since age 18 5.0% Last year 2.2%	3.5% 0.7%	SAQ following face-to-face interview	74%–78% (1988–1991)
Louis Harris & Associates, 1988 (Taylor, 1993)	739 men 409 women aged 16 to 50	Last 5 years 4.4% Last year 3.5% Last month 1.8%	3.6% 2.9% 2.1%	SAQ following face-to-face interview; same sex interviewer	67%

Study	Sample	Prevalence[1]		Method	Response rate
Research Triangle Institute (Rogers & Turner, 1991)	660 male residents of Dallas County, TX, aged 21–54	Last 10 years 8.1% Last year 4.6%	N/A N/A	SAQ	88%
National Survey of Men (NSM-1) (Billy et al., 1993)	3,321 men aged 20–39	Last 10 years 2.3%	N/A	Face-to-face interview; female interviewers	70%

NOTE: N/A=Not available

SAQ=Self-administered questionnaire

[1]Prevalence of male and female homosexuality calculated at RAND from General Social Surveys (Davis and Smith, 1991)

SOURCE: Reprinted by permission from Rand

▼ ▼

Dr. Kinsey's work, of course, does not cover consumer-related behavior nor does it reflect recent contemporary sexual values in men. It has also been criticized by others (besides the Rand Corporation) for its use of convenience sampling as opposed to random sampling.

Unfortunately, his contributions to this day continue to be erroneously used by the press and activists to make arguments (mainly the out-of-context use of the 10 percent figure) that simply do not apply to women.

The Janus Research, 1992

The Janus Report was published in 1993 by Samuel and Cynthia Janus.[8] It is a study derived from a substantially large sample size of 4,550 participants; of which 1,335 men and 1,384 women responded to questions regarding "homosexual experiences."

Each respondent was presented with anonymous questionnaires concerning "homosexual experiences" (research suggests an increased likelihood of disclosure when anonymity is allowed); and each participant was given the opportunity to "identify" as either homosexual or bisexual in addition to revealing specific sexual behavior.

The Janus report was not released early enough to be included in Rand's "Sexual Orientation and U.S. Military Personnel Policy," but conclusions are not likely to have changed Rand's final report in any significant way.

In the Janus study, participants were given a face-to-face personal interview prior to being handed an anonymous questionnaire with more controversial questions. Some researchers have suggested that this process may have created suspicion in participants' response to sensitive questions within the anonymous questionnaire.

In general, however, the Janus Report is among the most important and most significant of contemporary sexual research. When considered in its entirety, the findings may provide some insight to gay and lesbian consumer behavior.

The report concluded that 22 percent of males and 17 percent of females claimed having experienced at least one same-sex encounter in their lives. Of those responding, 9 percent of males *identified* as being homosexual or bisexual and 5 percent of females as being homosexual or bisexual.

▼ ▼

The Guttmacher Institute Research, 1992

The Alan Guttmacher Institute conducted a study entitled "The Sexual Behavior of Men in the United States," analyzed by the Battelle Research Center, which was released in 1992.[9] Although the study was not conducted specifically to determine the number of self-identified gay men in the United States or even the incidence of male-to-male sexual contact, it still received much play in the media because of one of its controversial conclusions that only 1 percent of its participants identified themselves as being gay.

This conclusion was not surprising, since most of the respondents were approached door to door in mainly suburban areas of the United States where gay and lesbian Americans are least likely to disclose their sexual identities.

Rivendell Marketing & the Simmons Research, 1994

Rivendell Marketing is a highly specialized firm of national advertising representatives with a solid track record in the domestic gay and lesbian marketplace. In association with a number of gay and lesbian newspapers, Rivendell contracted Simmons Market Research to investigate the psychographic backgrounds of gay and lesbian readers who regularly read publications represented nationally by Rivendell. This particular research is still tracked today by Simmons in association with Rivendell Marketing.

The gay and lesbian publications participating in the most recent Simmons study (conducted in February 1992) have formed a network called the National Gay Newspaper Guild, which has been in existence since 1988.[10] The NGNG is comprised of gay and lesbian publications across the United States including the *Bay Area Reporter* (San Francisco), *Bay Windows* (Boston), *Frontiers* (LA), *Dallas Voice, Houston Voice, New York Native, Philadelphia Gay News, Washington Blade* (DC), *The Weekly News* (Florida), and *Windy City Times* (Chicago).

In addition to the NGNG network, Rivendell Marketing, launched over fifteen years ago by the late Joe DiSabato, a former music industry promotions specialist, represents over 150 other important gay and lesbian publications in the United States—many of which have conducted independent research of their own readerships.

▼ ▼

Gay and lesbian newspaper publishing grew enormously during the 1970s, and by the beginning of the 1980s, every major American city had a least one regularly published gay and lesbian news publication. Several had two. Rivendell Marketing was influential in helping keep a number of these gay and lesbian publications visible among national advertising media buyers.

Some agencies launched large campaigns with Rivendell, including one for the movie *Making Love*, one of the first major American films to deal with homosexuality in a fair and altruistic manner, and a campaign for pharmaceutical company Merck Sharp Dome in the promotion of its new hepatitis vaccine. There were even focus groups conducted for what was then called the Gay and Lesbian Press Association.

Rivendell Marketing has provided advertisers and publishers with a much needed service in gay and lesbian advertising—allowing interested advertisers to reach the news-oriented gay and lesbian publishing market quickly and efficiently, and likewise helping local gay and lesbian news publications to make themselves known as a group in a more national way to the New York media and advertising world.

For a while, Rivendell Marketing also handled a sizable portion of advertising for the gay and lesbian telephone provider service industry (phone sex). Rivendell still handles "a fair amount" of this business, according to associate Michael Gravois, but he concedes that the industry's growth has probably "leveled off."

Rivendell Marketing's gross billings exceeded the one-million-dollar mark for the first time in 1990 and surged past two million the following year—in part because the marketplace was enjoying an explosion, but also because the pharmaceutical company Burroughs Wellcome had begun its controversial HIV-related advertising campaign in association with other groups—a campaign that encouraged people to get tested for the virus if they were among what were then termed "high-risk groups." Advertisements were displayed in many gay and lesbian publications and even in bus terminals in major cities across the United States.

Many read between the lines, though, and saw it as campaign to essentially promote the use of the drug AZT. The long-term efficacy of AZT's usefulness has been one of the single most hotly debated subjects among activists and individuals living with AIDS within the gay and lesbian community. But to date, Burroughs Wellcome has

▼ ▼

spent the single greatest amount of money in advertising for one integrated campaign in the gay and lesbian press.

The Simmons data, although often erroneously quoted by media and activists to represent the national gay and lesbian population as a whole, is one of the best representations of America's more afflu-ent gay and lesbian communities: readers of publications that are part of the National Gay Newspaper Guild.

Overlooked Opinions Research, 1990

Overlooked Opinions is a gay- and lesbian-oriented consumer research firm in Chicago. There's not sufficient reason to believe that any marketer would not benefit from at least testing the results culled from an Overlooked Opinion survey—especially since their researchers claim their participants to be so affluent.

However, the company has taken some criticism from within the gay and lesbian business community regarding their research con-clusions and their methodology—particularly over the $514 billion figure the firm has claimed as the size of the gay and lesbian econ-omy nationwide.

In an interview with an Overlooked Opinions associate who has since left the company, the database panel of participants was said to be over 200,000 (combined telephone and mail). Overlooked Opinions does not sell or rent its list of sample participants nor will they make available any of the names of the clients that have taken advantage of their services—which makes independent verification of their methodology problematic and, no doubt, has fueled the controversy over their numbers.

The controversy over Overlooked Opinions surrounds the $514 billion figure that was picked up and reported on by the national press and electronic media up until about 1993 without serious scrutiny and independent citing of other sources or opinions. When pressed on the legitimacy of the $514 billion number and how it was arrived at, Overlooked Opinions representatives said that they evaluated all the popular gay and lesbian research studies, including the 1990 Census data and a number of other factors—"but [essentially] formulated Kinsey's basic estimate of what he believed the gay and lesbian population size to be in association with a trade secret" that they weren't "interested in releasing."

Technically speaking, it is conceivable that the gay and lesbian mar-

Profile of the National Gay Newspaper Guild*

The National Gay Newspaper Guild (NGNG) is a network of gay publications from across the country that includes: *Bay Area Reporter* (San Francisco), *Bay Windows* (Boston), *Dallas Voice, Frontiers* (LA), *The New Voice* (Houston), *New York Native, Philadelphia Gay News, The Washington Blade* (DC), *The Weekly News* (Miami), and *Windy City Times* (Chicago).

Who Is the National Gay Newspaper Reader?

GENDER:	89.9% Male	
	10.1% Female	
AGE:	18–34	46.1%
	35–44	32.6%
	45–54	14.6%
EDUCATION:	59.6% graduated 4-year college or more	
EMPLOYMENT:	92.1% are employed	
	50.6% are professional/managerial	
	12.7% are employed in top management	
INCOME:	$41,300 Average individual income	
	53.9% have individual incomes over $30,000	
	21.7% have individual incomes over $50,000	
	$63,700 Average household income	
	79.2% have household incomes over $30,000	
	41.8% have household incomes over $60,000	

NATIONAL GAY NEWSPAPER GUILD READERSHIP STATISTICS:

Number of last 6 issues read or looked at	5.1 (mean)
Total amount of time spent with last issue	58.2 minutes
Total readers per copy	2.6
Combined NGNG circulations	229,250
Combined NGNG readerships	596,050

IMPACT ADVERTISEMENTS HAVE ON NGNG READERS:

Likely to use a product or service advertised	91.8%
Likely to purchase products or services of national businesses advertised	88.3%
Likelihood of mentioning to others products/services advertised in publication	49.8%

*The Profile of the NGNG readership is the exclusive property of the National Gay Newspaper Guild. No use or quotation of this study from its content may be made by anyone without the permission of a Guild member or an authorized representative.

SOURCE: Reprinted by permission from Rivendell Marketing

▼ ▼

ket does in fact comprise tens of billions of dollars annually, if all forms of financial activity are considered. And since the African-American and Hispanic consumer markets are currently rated in hundreds of billions, there is not sufficient reason to believe that Overlooked Opinions' "trade secret" should necessarily be divulged just to alleviate what may be nothing more than competitive grumbling within the gay and lesbian business community. But, as stated earlier, the Kinsey representation of 10 percent is technically erroneous when applied to women. Moreover, the $514 billion claim cannot be proven. However, one client of Overlooked Opinions who spoke only upon agreement of anonymity expressed that Overlooked Opinions' work for their firm was "especially thorough, timely, and enlightening."

At a recent Overlooked Opinions presentation of their services to the New York Advertising and Communications Network (one of the largest gay and lesbian professional organizations in the United States), the president Jeff Vitale was met with questioning from audience members regarding the $514 billion figure. His response was ambiguous, and after the presentation, one attendant remarked, "I know obfuscation when I hear it." Another remarked that "he was just smart—he knows not to give away the store. . . ."

Many businesspeople in the gay and lesbian community are suspicious and especially annoyed when they hear religious and political fringe groups arguing that "gays and lesbians are affluent and not in need of special rights"—especially when such fringe groups have cited Overlooked Opinions' $514 billion as proof that gays and lesbians are not worthy of minority status. Overlooked Opinions' official reaction to such allegations that they had unwittingly helped the radical right's cause was terse: "It's not our fault; it's poor planning on behalf of the gay and lesbian nonprofit groups that have let the radical right set the agenda. . . ."

In the final analysis, Overlooked Opinions has compiled an impressive list of gay and lesbian Americans. But most of their participants have been obtained through convenience sampling (at gay and lesbian business establishments, parades, etc.). And as explained, convenience sampling does not give the most accurate picture of an entire population.

Still, Overlooked Opinions database and services cannot be easily overlooked by marketers interested in investigating all their options.

▼ ▼

The Voter News Service, 1992

On Election Day 1992 the Voter New Service polled Americans with written questionnaires that were provided anonymously to people participating in the voting process at 300 different randomly selected locations across the country. In this study, 3.7 percent of the men and 2.8 percent of the women were determined to be self-identified gay or lesbian Americans, with 70 percent claiming to have voted for Clinton.

Although the total polling sample was extremely high, the results could not be generalized to the entire population because not everyone votes in an election. There was also concern that not everyone participating in the poll may have gotten to the end of the questionnaire where the question concerning whether or not someone identified as being "gay/lesbian/bisexual" appeared. However, only the yes votes were counted.

One of the most interesting findings in the final report indicated that "all voters believe by over 2 to 1 that government should promote traditional family values, while gays and lesbians believe by 2 to 1 that government should not promote one set of values over another." In addition, the study found that "there were no differences between gays and lesbians on the condition of the economy and they both had the same resistance to an increase in taxes, although gays and lesbians were more willing to accept increases for better health care. Gays and lesbians were also found to be more likely to pay attention to the candidates' wives and the conventions. There was also evidence that gays and lesbians were more active in the 1992 campaign than heterosexuals and were three times as likely to wear a campaign button.

The National Health and Social Life Survey, 1992

The National Health and Social Life Survey was conducted in 1992 by the National Opinion Research Center at the University of Chicago. With a random sample of 3,432 U.S. residents, the survey found 2.8 percent of the men and 1.4 percent of the women self-identifying as being gay.

This study found what other studies such as the Yankelovich MONITOR Gay and Lesbian Perspective and Simmons Market Research surveys found: that gay men and lesbians are more likely to self-identify in cities. This particular survey found that 10.2 per-

▼ ▼

cent more men and 2.1 percent more women were likely to self-identify in the 12 largest metropolitan areas of the country than in the suburbs.

Quotient, a national gay and lesbian marketing newsletter reported in the spring of 1995 that "the total number of respondents who self-identified as a gay or lesbian, who had felt desire for a same-sex partner and who had acted on that desire was only 23 women and 34 men." They further reported that the sample was "too small to make any conclusions about subgroups of the total," and that "one-fifth of the interviewees were interviewed in the presence of a partner or child which may have significantly reduced the honesty of their responses."

Newsweek Poll, 1994

The principal research for this poll was handled by Princeton Research Associates for a feature article in *Newsweek* entitled "Gay Power, Politics and Issues." Participants for this study, over 1,400 lesbians and gay men, were obtained through a random sampling of a gay and lesbian population database owned and managed by Strubco, New York City.

The poll found that over 70 percent of gay and lesbian Americans self-identifying as being gay or lesbian also claimed to be Democrats, with nearly 80 percent indicating they voted for Clinton. Unfortunately, the sample from which the participants were drawn is probably biased because it is largely composed of individuals who have given to gay and lesbian charities or who have purchased products from gay/lesbian-identified or -owned companies, thereby skewing the sample in a more affluent direction, just as Overlooked Opinions panel participants were also more likely to test out upscale.

The Overall Picture

Although other important studies do exist on gay and lesbian sexuality, they contribute little toward understanding gay and lesbian Americans qualitatively as consumers. For instance, the National Opinion Research Center in Chicago conducted a number of surveys between 1988 and 1992 that included questions about homo-

▼ ▼

sexuality, yet many refused to respond to questions about sexuality. Other studies conducted by universities and political think tanks may have contributed greatly to our understanding of sexuality, but none call into question the quantitative debates over gay and lesbian population size any more than those indicated above.

To date, the single most applicable and verifiable national gay and lesbian consumer population figure, based on random sampling conducted in the home by a widely respected commercial research firm in the United States and weighted against the 1992 census data, is by far the 1994-issued Yankelovich MONITOR Gay and Lesbian Perspective. In that study it was clearly demonstrated for marketers that gay and lesbian Americans are willing to self-identify as being gay or lesbian, if asked, at levels as high as 9 percent in large cities, and 2 percent to 4 percent in rural and suburban areas. This gives us a total self-identified national gay and lesbian population average of about 6 percent in the United States.

Setting the numbers debate aside, it is the qualitative information contained within the Yankelovich MONITOR Gay and Lesbian Perspective that marketers should be most enthusiastic about. This tells us new information about gay and lesbian purchasing behavior and what motivates and informs that process.

The study also reveals compelling and important developments that are taking place within the national gay and lesbian community—a community totaling a minimum of 15 million self-identified American consumers who are looking for new products and services produced by modern, contemporary-thinking companies willing to support them in their quest for upholding traditional values—traditional *American* values.

The Yankelovich MONITOR Gay and Lesbian Perspective, 1994

In the summer of 1993, I proposed that a number of institutions (including universities and advertising agencies) consider conducting an intensive, ground-breaking study on the rapid emergence of gay and lesbian consumerism in America. It was a study that would have to be based on nationally conducted focus groups or a battery of randomly selected respondents who could be scientifically gener-

▼ ▼

alized to the national population. It would investigate and analyze, for the first time, the extraordinary nature of gay and lesbian consumer and cultural attitudes in America, rather than the mere incidence of a particular kind of sexual behavior.

The methodology and handling of the research had to be high profile enough that anyone familiar with marketing science would see its immediate value and widespread application in business—particularly in tracking consumer perceptions. It had to have a usefulness to large corporations like AT&T and General Motors, but it also needed to intrigue gay and lesbian activists as well as generate interest in academic circles.

Yankelovich Partners, Inc., turned out to be the company willing to listen, investigate, and take the action necessary to get the job done. In June of 1994, the first Yankelovich MONITOR Perspective on Gays/Lesbians was completed and made commercially available. No other report or study of gay and lesbian Americans, as consumers, has ever been conducted like the one accomplished by Yankelovich. The final report may not be an infallible document, but for gay and lesbian Americans it is nothing less than a historical accomplishment. And for American business, particularly for marketers, it is a much awaited and long-needed high-tech instrument now confirming that the adult gay and lesbian population in the United States is a distinct, influential, and well-identified consumer group.

The Yankelovich investigation into gay and lesbian consumer motivations set a significant market precedent, but it also demonstrates why more research needs to be conducted. In many ways, the Yankelovich study has helped unmask the social myths surrounding gay and lesbian people—allowing more people in business to better discern what gay and lesbian consumers of this century want from the companies with which they do business. Today, it is specifically the increasing visibility of gays and lesbians—both in the media and the workplace—in combination with a growing portfolio of new research about them that is allowing the remaining myths of the twentieth century to evaporate. In fact, it was this increased visibility in the marketplace that helped bring about Yankelovich Partners' acknowledgment that such a study should be conducted.

Now, rather than dredging through the remaining vestiges of gay and lesbian population debates and stereotypes, business and gov-

▼ ▼

ernment is better served by an investigation into how the effects of such myths have commercially segregated gays and lesbians as individual consumers and influenced the way in which they are now participating in the economy. To help understand the major distinctions between self-identified gay and lesbian consumers and heterosexual consumers, a brief summary of the social climate currently prevalent among the total population of American consumers is provided in the next chapter. This information—which has been tracked since 1971—is part of an ongoing study by Yankelovich Partners, known as the Yankelovich MONITOR, that businesses both in the United States and all over the world turn to regularly for sophisticated analysis and unique perspective of American consumer behavior.

The underlying methodological assumption of the MONITOR is that traditional economic and demographic predictors such as those tracked by the government are insufficient for a complete understanding of marketplace behavior. Therefore, in addition to measuring traditional demographics, the Yankelovich MONITOR is designed to quantitatively measure social attitudes, values, perceptions, and behaviors thus sketching a more complete portrait of the consumer.

The Yankelovich MONITOR research cited in this book (and the Yankelovich MONITOR Perspective on Gays/Lesbians as originally conducted for this book), was collected by means of a 90-minute, personal interview conducted in the homes of a representative national sample of 2,500 consumers over the age of 16. Interviewing was conducted door-to-door in 315 locations across the continental United States and is balanced (weighted) to mirror U.S. Census demographic characteristics.

To provide a broad picture of what is going on in the minds of American consumers, the Yankelovich MONITOR covers a wide variety of subjects, many of them extremely sensitive. In order to insure accurate information on these issues, a number of techniques are constructed to alleviate embarrassment or anxiety on the part of Yankelovich's respondents. Two are particularly worth noting:

- The one and one-half hour questionnaire is administered in the respondent's home—a secure environment controlled by the respondent.
- Sensitive topics, such as those dealing with individual identity,

are placed in a spiral binder of exhibit cards. For such questions, each respondent is instructed to turn to the appropriate card and asked to indicate only the number that corresponds to the responses chosen. In this way, respondents disclose information confidentially.

Regarding statistical significance and the gay/lesbian sample of the Yankelovich data cited here, approximately 6 percent of the 2,500 respondents 16 years of age and older is represented (n=148). Total error due to sampling is plus or minus 4 percent. The sample was identified by means of an item in the 1993 Yankelovich MONITOR participant interviews requiring respondents to choose from a list of 52 adjectives/phrases, items that the respondent believed best described them. The exact wording of the item used to identify respondents for this analysis was "gay/homosexual/lesbian."

Researchers at Yankelovich Partners indicate that, for marketers, this self-identification technique may be more reliable than others which have been used to analyze the gay/lesbian population. Magazine subscription lists or voluntary return mail questionnaires are neither random nor representative of the gay and lesbian population as a whole; they contain substantial bias and are not weighted to mirror U.S. Census demographic characteristics. The value of the Yankelovich data and methodology is that it has identified only those consumers who are willing to acknowledge that they are gay or lesbian, and it has scientifically identified them using a random sampling formula reflecting the entire population.

Further, Yankelovich respondents were not asked to divulge information about their sexual identity through a written questionnaire. Nor were they required to "check off any boxes" or write anything down on paper, or even answer any verbal questions about sexual behavior per se during the interview process. They were simply given the opportunity to identify themselves as being gay/lesbian/homosexual by citing a number associated with one of the 52 listed descriptors in the spiral binder.[11]

This sliver of difference in questioning and identifying gay and lesbian participants regarding sexual identification may well be the driving determinant that resulted in a higher percentage of gays and lesbians being indicated over more recent studies to date. In any event,

▼ ▼

the Yankelovich study did not seek to determine sexual behavior—
only self-disclosed sexual identity. Once the self-identified gay/les-
bian/homosexual individuals were determined, Yankelovich then
looked at what characteristics, attitudes, beliefs, and values separated
them from the overall sample—presumed to be largely heterosexual.

The conclusions are examined in the next chapter. Some of the
findings, frankly, were predictable. Most, however, are enlighten-
ing—and some are astonishing.

▼ ▼

CHAPTER 4

PRIDE AND PRAGMATISM

Understanding Gay and Lesbian Consumer Culture

A foolish consistency is the hobgoblin of little minds, adored by little statesmen and philosophers and divines.

RALPH WALDO EMERSON

As Americans, we are fed up with the complicated, the cluttered, and the entangled. We are no longer stimulated by our social environment. For many of us, the social environment is now perceived as threatening.

As a result, we have begun developing stronger and stronger desires to streamline the living process—to clear away what no longer serves us, is problematic, pervasive, useless, or filled with rigidity.

We want simplicity.[1]

In our desire to create more understanding, clarity, and comfort in our lives, a number of social and economic changes are making themselves painfully apparent: one of which is the wholesale disruption of the long-held sacrosanct institution of marriage.

In the past twenty-five years, heterosexual marriage has undergone enormous changes around the world. In the United States alone, the sheer numbers of people getting married and staying married is certifiably on the decline. The estimates vary, but the accepted divorce rate is now at about 50 percent. Getting out of a legal marriage is now literally as common as getting into one.

In 1975, roughly 500,000 heterosexuals claimed to be living together but unmarried. Today that number is a whopping six times

▼ ▼

larger, totaling over 3 million—as many as were merely "going steady" during the middle of the twentieth century.[2]

In addition, it is now no longer safe to say that *living together*, out of wedlock, is a fad. Fads only last a few seasons. Nor would it be altogether fair to refer to such developments as a "trend." Trends last several seasons.

America is experiencing an evolution in the status of heterosexual marriage—one of its most fundamental organizing principles of society. In fact, this is an evolution that is occurring worldwide—in both industrialized and developing countries. As the *New York Times* recently noted, "Around the world, in rich and poor countries alike, the structure of family life is undergoing profound changes, a new analysis of research from numerous countries has concluded. 'The idea that the family is a stable and cohesive unit in which father serves as economic provider and mother serves as emotional caregiver is a myth,' said Judith Bruce, an author of the study. 'The reality is that trends like unwed motherhood, rising divorce rates, smaller household and the feminization of poverty are not unique to America, but are occurring worldwide.' "[3]

One of the central forces behind these changes relates to the need for women to enter the workforce in order to continue providing a stable environment for children. In addition, cuts by governments to dependent families is an increasing trend around the globe as are cuts to education in an attempt to repay national debts to larger nations.

A report issued by the Population Council[4] entitled "Families in Focus" found that the stability of child support payments by fathers separated from children is also difficult to maintain in countries other than the United States. The report claimed "that among divorced fathers, three-quarters in Japan, almost two-thirds in Argentina, half in Malaysia and two-fifths in the United States do not pay child support."

As the report argued, there needs to be a rethinking of the "policies and programs to strengthen the father-child link. . . . "

With all these changes occurring at an accelerated pace in the United States, clearly an entirely new array of consequences are being placed at our national doorstep. Some positive. Some negative. Although many would argue more the latter.

The point? There are interesting parallels between the disruptions and stresses of marriage in America and the isolation and

▼ ▼

stresses experienced by gay and lesbian people living in a predominantly heterosexual society.

Americans are all facing major changes related to economics; some we understand, many we are still seeking answers for. Obviously, wherever one is financially situated within the economic structure is where one experiences the effects of the economy, which does not always make for pleasant encounters among the citizenry. But first, before more closely investigating gay and lesbian economics, a few considerations should be explored in general about the evolution of all Americans and their values in relation to sex and money.

Economics and the Sexual Identity Crisis

As healthy human organisms interacting within what is still our evolving experiment in free enterprise, we are constantly responding and reacting to a number of social stimuli, including—perhaps most devisively—the commercial politics related to keeping the American individual's mind centered on the idea that the attainment of wealth is necessarily a "good thing."

Perhaps it is, or could one day be made to be. But I argue that the waning of heterosexual commitment to marriage and all that it entails is as much related to the demands of the modern economic state and our perpetual need to attain wealth than any new notion of the abandonment of ideals as delivered by Moses and stylized by modern cable televangelism.

The twentieth century has inflicted upon the American psyche nearly all possible stresses imaginable. We are now subconsciously trying to find ways to alleviate the pressure to get rich by seeking out new forms of expression—new ways of strengthening and reinventing human identity, democratic idealism, and "the pursuit of happiness." This search for more applicable values is particularly noticeable in the angry but fresh new rhetoric and searing expansive vision of America's younger gay and lesbian citizens.

In the meantime, everything from Prohibition, Depression, world war, postwar population growth; McCarthyism, class, race, and sexual wars; the Vietnam War, Star Wars, the Gulf War, media wars, culture wars, media expansion, media mergers, media monopolies, the monopolization of commercial culture, inflation, recession, obsession, the destruction of community culture, commercialized electronic churches, information superhighway, and the forever altered feeling and meaning behind the name *Oklahoma* have been rained down upon the American public's living room. Now, as we look to the next century, we are dealing with an unpredictable and threatening world economy that is allowing the price of everything from dishpans and telephones to hairstyling perm rods and electrical extension cords to be determined in some neo-totalitarian sweatshop deep in the heart of China.

Today, with everyone working—men, women, teenagers (gay or straight)—the regimental product-laden household of yesteryear has been left literally abandoned in postmodern suburbia. Man is no longer head of household. Woman is no longer a subordinate homemaking entity. Children are no longer purposefully conceived and raised to help "man the farm" or run the "family business." What were once traditional household systems of the nineteenth and twentieth century are now outmoded excursions into nostalgia partitioned off to the land of the television rerun. The old economic paradigms are wearing out. And so are many of the old notions of what constitutes a family.

Today we are said to be more informed, but at the same time more commercially exploited than any previous generation. This has been brought on by the twenty-four-hour availability of commercial media, which constantly paws at our heartstrings and purse strings, telling us we need what we haven't got, whether we require it or not.

Our cumulative waking hours are also now spent differently—looking and responding to more aggressive, more commercialized, often coded imagery. The images we see in advertising, television, and films affect us greatly. They contribute to our increased levels of stress and guilt about our individual worth—even our relationship to the world's problems. And as we all work harder than the generation before us, we awaken to find our money less valuable and the continued earning of it more problematic. We sense economic vulnerability both through experience and through media. We have social stresses, demands, health concerns, costs, and procedures that our parents didn't have. Our children know more about drugs, sex, and guns than we do. They drink, drug, and struggle more with sex than we did. We're told that we can't trust our senses, that we can no longer eat what tastes good to us. We're even required by law to sort our trash differently.

▼ ▼

The feeling we are left with is something I call "hypercomplexity"—a subtle, modern kind of socioeconomically based fear. One that at times manifests itself among some people as something cunning, baffling, and powerful; among others as confusion that is hard to identify. But it is ubiquitous. It exists among our families and in our institutions. We see it on the streets and in shopping center parking lots. We notice it in restaurants, we feel it on Sunday afternoon after watching the morning news shows. We anticipate alleviating it when traffic doesn't move. We feel it when the answering machine isn't blinking with a message when we get home, just as we feel it when it's blinking. We feel it when we we're uncertain about a product we're buying. We feel it even more when we try to understand the label.

If today's families are going to stick together (no matter how they are fashioned), they are going to have to find new ways to deal with hypercomplexity—new ways of dealing with social and economic fear based on a more primary purpose than the attainment of wealth.

Patriarchal-based consumer economic units and family values rhetoric don't deal with hypercomplexity in modern America; they make it worse.

Adaptation and Change

Gay and lesbian Americans are masters at dealing with hypercomplexity. This is because they grow up learning to deal with fear, repression, and raised eyebrows every single day of their lives.

As children many are taunted and abused; others are quietly put in their place by silences or polite pauses in conversations. As the historian James M. Saslow, who wrote *Ganymede in the Renaissance: Homosexuality in Art and Society,* expressed in an interview with veteran *Advocate* journalist Mark Thompson, "I was a bookworm, not the least bit interested in sports, and very creative. . . . The word everybody always used to describe me was artistic. But there would be this slight pause before they said it, so I knew they weren't just talking about my ability to draw. There was something larger the word seemed to refer to, but people would never quite say it out loud."[5]

Most gay and lesbian Americans go through a period of time when they have trouble finding common ground with their parents and

▼ ▼

church leaders. Puberty is often a nightmare. For some, high school feels like a concentration camp. And until the 1990s, gay and lesbian celebrity role models and public examples were nonexistent.

Under such conditions, gay and lesbian emotional coping systems become so keenly fine-tuned, warlike, and powerful that self-defense, individual freedom, and high moral ground become the reason for living. Which is why one of the most progressive, wide-scale responses to the fears and social frictions currently occurring within the economic fabric of our society is most easily recognized among gay and lesbian Americans and their individually formulated communities, families, and social institutions. Because these have been built out of sheer self-defense against what is perceived as a historically vexatious heterosexual environment.

In looking at gay and lesbian social and consumer behavior, I do not propose that gay and lesbian communities have all the answers to America's economically-based social problems. But a simple fact cannot be denied: gay and lesbian Americans have never fit nor been allowed into traditional patriarchal society, and as a result, they have had no choice but to create their own. And therein lies the crux of understanding gay and lesbian consumerism—particularly the rhetoric and actions of young gay and lesbian Americans.

Traditionally, gay and lesbian individuals throughout history have been denied the right to participate in the majority of state-and church-sanctioned institutions and rituals—because such social monuments were designed to insure the viability of heterosexually organized economic systems, their livelihood and longevity, and to isolate anything that does not conform.

No doubt, much has changed. But in the United States, gay and lesbian Americans are still not federally protected from discrimination in employment, housing, insurance, or military service. Gay and lesbian Americans do not enjoy the same number of equal protections under the law as heterosexuals do.

The reason for this is simple: Gay and lesbian Americans are not heterosexual, not part of what was once a reigning decree of social order, the paradigm on which our economy has been organized for so long.

When gay and lesbian Americans travel abroad, they're often shocked to learn the degree to which they find gay and lesbian people from other countries enjoying more civil rights and legal pro-

▼ ▼

tections than they do as Americans. This is particularly so in Holland, Sweden, Denmark—and most recently, South Africa, which now contains the words *sexual orientation* in its new constitution.

Gay and lesbian Americans are well aware that many heterosexual Americans have gravely misunderstood the degree to which the real democratic values of America have begun to fade—because straight people in our country are seldom called upon to experience the erosion of basic human rights from the gay/lesbian communities' perspective.

It is especially interesting (actually, ominous) that gay and lesbian Americans are routinely accused by political extremists as asking for special rights and perpetuating a "homosexual agenda"—and as has been stated, often blamed or scapegoated for our country's alleged decline of moral values and crumbling of family structures. Yet gay men and lesbians were never accepted as part of such structures to begin with.

For sure, gay and lesbian Americans laugh at such folly. But they are enraged by it as well. The talk of the breakup of the family has been going on in the American press dating back as far as 1831 with the "new moral reform movements."[6] During those times, there were even "societies" and "task forces" set up with the help of government to allegedly uphold traditional values, yet underground economies forged around alcoholism and prostitution were quietly encouraged to flourish—just as drugs and alcoholism are allowed to flourish today.

Even the tired twentieth-century lament "Just say no" originated from the early days of the nineteenth century[7]—yet few Americans realize it is just another coded statement revived 150 years later under Reaganomics.

Of course, the hollow efforts at reform of the early 1800s were largely a failure, just as they were a hundred years later during Prohibition, and as they are again, at the turn of this century. But with one exception: new, gay-and-lesbian-based economic paradigms have begun to emerge—paradigms based on the ongoing need for the gay and lesbian individual to adapt to history's war against gay and lesbian consumerism: the so-called homosexual agenda.

As heterosexual society focused on staying consistent throughout the years, gay and lesbian society remained spontaneous. It evolved,

▼ ▼

responded, organized, and began influencing everything from American arts and science to social politics, and now, consumer economics.

More Adaptation and More Change

Today, new ideas about consumer economic systems and how they affect the well-being of the individual are germinating in the experiences and psyches of gays and lesbians all across America. As a traditionally isolated people, gays and lesbians have had to custom-fashion and redirect their personal values and group understandings of the world toward a more common sense-oriented approach to modern life *as it really is for them*—out of sheer emotional and financial self-preservation.

As John D'Emilio wrote in *Sexual Politics, Sexual Communities: The Making of a Homosexual Minority in the United States, 1940–1970,*

> In addition to the opprobrium emanating from religion, law, and medicine, American society at large revealed its disapproval of homosexual eroticisim by sharply curtailing public discussion of the topic. . . .
>
> [Eventually] gay liberation affected the self-image even of those men and women who never joined a gay organization or participated in a demonstration. Its ideas permeated the subculture of lesbians and homosexuals so that pride and openness became common characteristics. . . . During the 1970s in virtually every area of American life, debates raged and battles were fought over homosexuality.[8]

With the passage of time—both before and since the 1970s—it is apparent just how many struggles and victories around sexual orientation have become intertwined with race and women's emancipation. In retrospect, the entire twentieth century is beginning to resonate with a theme that is infused with the passion of gay and lesbian spirituality, independence, and dignity. It is apparent in the dynamic fabric and now unfolding truth about gay and lesbian influence and its importance during the Harlem Renaissance, the anti-war movement, the 1960s civil rights movement, the Daughters of Bilitis and the Mattachine Society's impact over a decade before the Stonewall Riots, the subtle lifting of consciousness brought on by the Radical Fairies and the Women's Music Movement, Disco, and now, most recently, the

▼ ▼

AIDS crisis, ACT-UP, Queer Nation, Lesbian Avengers, and the sheer noise level of *Outweek* magazine—a forerunner in the explosive growth of gay and lesbian-centered media.

Provocative and revolutionary? Yes.

In gay and lesbian America, family is not dead. It is evolving and responsive. It is growing. It is powerfully alive, vibrant, moral, and generative. And has been all through this century. But today it is simply more visible, amplified, and willing to create dynamic, economically based coalitions. It is focused on individuality, diversity, affirmative opportunity, and a deep moral sense of balance between the civic, the spiritual, the environmental, and the economic. It would be genuinely hard to find a more deeply passionate group of people more staunchly dedicated to the values of democracy and free enterprise than those within the gay and lesbian community in America today.

The gay and lesbian consumer revolution is at once both Madisonian and Jeffersonian in its textbook defense of free enterprise and simultaneous call for federal government to uphold their rights in housing and employment based on sexual identity. Untold millions of dollars in industry profits are now at risk for American businesses that do not take seriously the vibrancy and power of gay and lesbian productivity and influence in American culture, business innovation, and corporate management philosophy. At its best, the gay and lesbian consumer revolution in America will be about the quiet sharing of consumer product information in relationship to, and in concordance with, the public trading of stocks based on a corporation's social behavior in the workplace and in the global marketplace. The modern gay and lesbian consumer revolution is about responsible, informed Americans, activist-minded, and unswervingly committed to the most original of American ideals.

This is not the "Me Generation" revisited. It is a wholesale rediscovery of one of our most original American values—that of individualism—a total shifting of the focus of responsibility away from outdated *family* structures back to *individual* structures—as envisioned during the early days of our republic: Freedom of the individual. Freedom of enterprise. Civic responsibility. Equal protection under the law.

Sound familiar? Republican? Democratic? Yes. The gay and lesbian consumer revolution is all of these things.

▼ ▼

But with one exception: the age of the patriarchal-based consumer society is over.

And standing in its wake from Greenwich Village to Orange County, from the San Francisco Castro to the congressional district of Jesse Helms lies the archetypal beginning of a much more *free* and *enterprising* democratic system. A system based on a more stringent level of equal protection under the law, held in check and balance by the marketplace and the new hyper-informed consumer.

If American business is willing to change, it will be amazed before the profits begin to be shared. American business is going to realize a new level of marketing and customer service based on a reinvented norm of American idealism—individuality. American business need not fear backlash or wish to hide its relationship with gay and lesbian consumers—because gay and lesbian consumers are all about working with business for the betterment of life—as opposed to the exploitation of it.

The gay and lesbian consumer revolution in America is an evolutionary system that is already working, with business, perhaps your competition, for change—change that is good for everyone. Because the new age of consumer individuality is all about inclusivity, affirmative opportunity, and civic responsibility.

This revolution is also pragmatic, morally driven, willing to boycott—and unstoppable.

Context Matters

To fully understand gay and lesbian consumerism in modern America, we must first take inventory of what is going on in the hearts and minds of the American consumer population—both gay and straight. This must be done based on the best possible scientific analysis—devoid of Cracker Jack moralizing and free of intolerant political rhetoric and double-talk marketplace messaging.

Bearing this in mind, it is important to acknowledge that for some time radical right-wing extremists have been calling for a "cultural war"—claiming that the "breakup of the family" is largely related to our abandoning of traditional values as a nation. At the same time they are spreading coded messages through media in an effort to discredit or blame societal problems on racial, sexual, and economic minorities—particularly gay and lesbian Americans.

▼ ▼

To help keep matters within their proper context, the Yankelovich MONITOR research data in this chapter is presented in two parts. The first addresses the social temperature and environment for the entire American population. The second part addresses how gay and lesbian Americans appear to differ from the population as a whole.[9]

I: A SOCIAL CLIMATE OVERVIEW OF ALL AMERICANS

Before looking at what is driving the gay and lesbian consumer revolution in America, it is important to understand what characteristics currently make up the values, beliefs, and concerns of the overall population—meaning both gay and straight, as a national group, the overall American citizenry.

Yankelovich Partners routinely conducts research in this area and compiles its findings and analysis in a social climate overview. In looking at the Yankelovich overview, the following attitudinal and demographic trends among all Americans were sighted as being of primary importance in the *current social context* of American life:[10]

1: AMERICANS: THEIR CONFIDENCE AND TRUST

In the early 1990s there was the feeling in the country that our institutions let us down. This included consumer confidence in government, the economy, the medical establishment, military, business, and more. There was concern that such institutions would continue to decline. The consumer's attitudes toward business was a dichotomy—there was an atmosphere of uncertainty about the future, yet consumers yearned for someone to trust. And despite environmental factors that have remained the same to a large degree, consumers seem to be turning the corner and are more ready to stop playing the "Blame Game." They are demanding more accountability and responsibility for actions of both themselves and of others. The following should particularly be noted:

- On one hand, people have faith in the ability of American business to compete internationally.
- On the other hand, there is a sense that business victimizes individuals—both consumers (with bad products and high prices) and employees (with layoffs, wage cuts, and poor management). Trust in advertising is still at a crisis level.

- An opportunity exists for companies to differentiate themselves as trustworthy and concerned about the needs of others. In general, people are increasingly demonstrating trust in themselves above trust in anyone else.
- Companies and brands can stand out as shining examples of strong performance by providing the basics: good quality, reasonable prices, consistency, reliability, and honest communication.

2: AMERICAN PRIVACY, FEAR OF CRIME, AND THE NEED TO CONNECT

Basically consumers are moving into what they feel is the unknown. They perceive that this area of the unknown will offer them few guarantees. There is also increased fear and concern about crime, violence, and privacy as they become more focused on their overall safety. An overwhelming majority of consumers now agree that crime is the most serious problem facing the country. This was particularly pronounced among women. There are also many more concerns about privacy and maintaining individual rights. Nonetheless, for the first time in years, consumers are eager to make plans for the future as a way of gaining control over their lives. But the lack of confidence in traditionally reliable institutions and ideologies make planning still a major challenge. Consumers are now searching for ways to reach out and connect. In addition:

- Today's consumers believe there is no way to tell how much money will be required for personal retirement funds or children's education, yet family is reemerging and children appear to be more appreciated and treasured.
- People are wondering how education and retirement can be defined and applied in the future.
- People are looking for trusted companions for life's journey as they look for an increasing sense of community obligation and commitment.
- People are also looking for new options that can help them meet new challenges.

3: RESTRAINED SPENDING

With or without recession, consumers have downgraded their wants from the spending spree of the 1980s. They still buy what they want, but they want less and there is no sense of sacrifice when

▼ ▼

they do without. "Economizing" involves things that don't really matter and "what matters" is no longer determined by the opinions of others. The country's recent recession was not the only cause of restrained spending:

- It produced caution rather than panic and more sensible spending patterns, including efforts to reduce debt.
- It indicated that no "pent-up demand" is likely to appear in the near future, suggesting that spending will continue at current levels.

In addition, American consumers have adopted a new restraint about purchasing, which helps them control spending:

- "Instant gratification" has given way to waiting for the "right moment," when the price is right.
- If what they want is not available or not at the right price, they may often substitute from another category.

4: CONTINUED NEED FOR STREAMLINING AND SIMPLIFICATION

Today, complexity is seen as threatening and exhausting. Yet consumers' daily lives continue to be crowded with tasks. This is creating a demand for the simplification of some task and the complete abandonment of others.

With regard to shopping and the associated purchase decisions, consumers are seeking to streamline their involvement. Today, consumers are:

- Buying what works and what meets their expectations.
- Not necessarily pursuing the newest or best.
- Reducing their interest in the often complicated and frustrating promotional "game."
- Finding reliable, useful information—often from other consumers.
- Using retail outlets that have provided successful results in the past.

5: FUN AND THE NEED FOR RELAXATION AND STRESS RELIEF

The best way to describe what today's consumers are feeling in relationship to the street could be summed up as "Life is tough, we need some fun."

In our increasingly competitive and demanding world, consumers are seeking continual relief from stress. Fun and fantasy offer positive and healthy distractions for escaping the daily grind. But even the distraction can, at times, prove more stressful:

- Consumers seek to share their leisure experiences with others by taking part in rituals, "community" activities, and religion.
- But often the escape is solitary, because other people can also be a source of stress by the demands they make. There is the need to "make my own fun."

6: REDUCED HEALTH AND FITNESS CONCERNS

Enough is enough. As consumers, we are continuing to care about nutrition, weight, etc., but we are no longer obsessed with these issues. We have adjusted our diets and exercise schedules, but we are tired of "healthy eating."

Food and drink are perceived to be among the few remaining safe pleasures available in life. In addition, concern about all specific health issues is declining. This is not necessarily because we have taken care of these concerns, but because people simply refuse to worry about them all the time. Therefore:

- Good taste is now the most important benefit.
- Low calorie and fat content appears to have become a ticket of entry in many categories, but one that will occasionally be ignored in the pursuit of good taste. Control is maintained via frequency of consumption rather than by sacrifice of taste.
- Nutrition, calories, fat grams, and the rest are now secondary concerns.

7: A FRAGMENTING CONSUMER MARKETPLACE

Two important areas that will be discussed below are impacting on America's changing consumer landscape. The first concerns the three *generational views* of life in the 1990s. The second concerns the changing racial and ethnic background of the United States population.

8: AMERICANS AND THE ACCEPTANCE OF THE ROLE OF TECHNOLOGY

Technological products are a fact of life for most consumers, as they continue to have expectations that these types of products should simplify their lives. Technology, however, becomes a major issue for the majority of consumers if something goes wrong. There is increased expectation not only for high technology, but for high performance.

Looking at America's Three Generational Views of Life

Key areas of focus and concern among Americans are interpreted differently based on age and the associated historical experiences related to age. This has resulted in the evolutionary development of three distinct consumer population cohorts in the United States: the Mature Generation; Baby Boomers; and the so-called Generation X. Each of these groups contribute to the fragmenting process within the American consumer marketplace spectrum. Each group's world-view varies according to its own social and economic acculturational process within history.

Regarding their marketplace perspective, each of the three generations differ greatly—not only in their worldview, but their marketplace behavior as well. The groups are best characterized in the following way:

- The Mature Generation (age 50 and up) grew up with the memories of the Depression and two world wars that taught them caution, thrift, playing by the rules, and living for tomorrow. Matures buy the "right thing," what someone "like me" is expected to have. Gender distinctions remain clear for them; women are responsible for shopping and all food and beverage decisions. Structure and order is important to them; change is perceived as threatening.
- The Baby Boomer generation (ages 30–49) grew up in an era of unparalleled prosperity and possibilities from which they developed a psychology of entitlement and a "can-do" attitude that does not recognize limits. Boomers continue to focus on selecting "what's right for me." They believe, with reason, that products are made and marketed to meet their own personal needs. Their current life stage makes them among the most stressed consumers (jobs *and* kids *and* personal lives). Leisure and relaxation are therefore particularly important to them.

▼ ▼

- Generation X (ages 16–29) has faced a difficult economy and a fiercely competitive environment throughout their lives. They have grown up to have a practical, cynical, and self-protective nature. Generation Xers worry about being able to get what they want and need, but they are ready to do what they must to succeed in the marketplace, as well as in other aspects of life. They feel that they "get no respect" from the marketplace, which focuses on the needs of the two previous generations. Xers are extremely worried about their personal future, especially their ability to find and maintain a job. Many have adopted a "live for today" attitude, especially with regard to leisure and fun, since the opportunities of today may not be available tomorrow.

Race and Ethnicity in America: A Melting Pot No Longer

Along with the three generational views of American consumers come cultural and economic dynamics that impact on the fragmentation of the marketplace. These dynamics are informed, in part, by issues relating to race and ethnicity. For instance, African-Americans will remain a constant 12 percent of the population; however, the Asian and Hispanic segments of the U.S. population will grow rapidly, both by birth and immigration.

Considered together, this will mean one out of three Americans will belong to a "minority" group ten years after the turn of the century.

This development signals changes for everything, from music and entertainment to food, cooking, and other characteristics of modern life that impact upon mainstream American culture (for instance, salsa now outsells ketchup in the United States).

In addition, today's immigrant populations, unlike earlier waves, have a different approach to assimilation. They wish to become American and to enjoy all the rights and responsibilities that this entails. But they also desire to retain key elements of their national culture—most important, their native language.

Bearing all these varying issues in mind—that gay and lesbian Americans also fit into Mature, Baby Boomer, and Generation X cohorts, and that they also contribute and respond to issues relating to the overall social climate, race, ethnicity, age, and experience—we are now ready to examine the emerging gay and lesbian attitudinal mind-set in modern America.

▼ ▼

II: THE MAKING OF A MODERN GAY AND LESBIAN AMERICAN PROFILE

With the research conducted by Yankelovich Partners, it is now possible to better understand gay and lesbian consumers on a number of scientific, social, and economic frontiers. The first important phase of this research, completed in the summer of 1994, was conducted in collaboration for this book and based on the scientific analysis of a variety of social values among research respondents who identified themselves as being "gay, lesbian, or homosexual" in the Yankelovich 1993 population study sample. Yankelovich researchers monitor approximately fifty different social values among research participants from year to year. They then follow and interpret what these social values and their fluctuations can mean in relationship to the consumer's ideas and behaviors.

What follows is a review of what Yankelovich researchers were able to discern about gay and lesbian Americans, their views, their ideas, and how they differ from the overall, predominantly heterosexual, population. In addition, several revealing charts and tables have been included to assist the reader in grasping the degree to which American gay and lesbian individuals might react to various forms of marketing in ways different from heterosexuals. These charts show the percentages of gay/lesbian respondents who responded to Yankelovich MONITOR questioning in relation to the heterosexual sample. Although there was an entire range of data tracked by the Yankelovich MONITOR in 1993, only the data for which there were highly significant differences is included here.

Understanding the Data: Statistical Significance

Differences between the gay/lesbian population and the general population that are statistically significant at the 95 percent confidence level are shown in each chart as follows:

- Positive differences are indicated by a clear box.
- Negative differences are indicated by a shaded box.
- Numbers not boxed do not represent statistically significant differences from the general population. That is to say, differences observed could have occurred due to chance.

▼ ▼

Gay and Lesbian Americans: Understanding the Big Picture

Gay and lesbian American consumers exhibit key areas of difference and alikeness when compared to the population as a whole. Accepting, responding to, and making use of this information is critical to the process of understanding and engaging modern gay and lesbian consumer culture. These differences and resemblances also play an important role in helping marketers to determine and develop effective niche-marketing approaches as well as more generalized advertising campaigns aimed at gay and lesbian consumer cohorts.

It is important to establish that the gay/lesbian sample in this report is *similar* to the heterosexual population in terms of age, gender ethnicity, occupation, employment, income, and formal political affiliation (although gays/lesbians generally espouse a more liberal viewpoint). However, the gay/lesbian population is *more likely* to have attended graduate school, be self-employed, and live in a large metropolitan area—this is particularly so in the Northeast.

The gay/lesbian sample is *less likely* than the heterosexual population to be Protestant, live in the South, be married, be parents (although 50 percent of gays/lesbians report being parents), or to live in a household where children under 18 are present (although 24 percent of gays/lesbians do).

We will first address the hard issues and core makeup of this consumer group's demographics. Then we will explore analysis pointing to five solid areas of difference as indicated in the research, followed by the Brigg's psychology of disenfranchisement.

Population Size

As stated in chapter 3, approximately 6 percent of the 1993 Yankelovich MONITOR sample identified themselves as "gay/lesbian/homosexual," a figure somewhere between the percentages reported in other studies (such as the Guttmacher Institute and the often-quoted-out-of-context Kinsey ranging from 1 percent to 10 percent, respectively).

Age and Sex

The gay/lesbian population mirrors the heterosexual population's distribution in these characteristics:

▼ ▼▼ ▼▼ ▼▼ ▼▼ ▼▼ ▼▼ ▼▼ ▼▼ ▼▼ ▼▼ ▼▼ ▼▼ ▼▼ ▼▼ ▼▼ ▼▼ ▼▼ ▼▼ ▼

	Gay/Lesbian %	*Heterosexual* %
SEX:		
Male	44	48
Female	56	52
AGE:		
16–24	22	17
25–34	21	23
35–44	21	21
45–54	13	13
55–64	8	10
65+	15	16

Ethnicity

The gay/lesbian sample is evenly distributed throughout the population with regard to ethnicity, although there is a slightly above-average representation of Hispanics.

	Gay/Lesbian %	*Heterosexual* %
RACE:		
White	72	78
African-American	11	11
Spanish/Hispanic	13	8
Other Minority	4	3

Education

Level of education attainment is significantly higher for the gay/lesbian sample, particularly at the graduate school level. This demographic distinction is usually linked to substantially higher income levels as well as employment at the professional/executive level, although subsequent tables in this chapter will show that, contrary to recent media misinformation, this is not the case for the gay/lesbian population.

▼ ▼

	Gay/Lesbian %	Heterosexual %
LEVEL OF EDUCATION ATTAINED BY RESPONDENT:		
Less than 4 years of high school	20	26
High school graduate	31	37
ANY COLLEGE (NET)	49	37
Less than 4 years	23	19
College graduate	12	11
Graduate school	14	7

Employment and Occupation

There were no significant differences found in the broad demographic categories of employment and occupation, except that gays/lesbians are more likely to be self-employed. This fact is particularly worth noting since business-to-business marketing approaches aimed at gay and lesbian individuals is relatively nonexistent. Many opportunities to reach gay and lesbian businesspeople exist through gay and lesbian business and trade organizations and gay and lesbian business publications and newsletters

	Gay/Lesbian %	Heterosexual %
EMPLOYED (NET):	**62**	**62**
Part time	15	13
Full time	47	49
SELF-EMPLOYED	18	**11**
OCCUPATION:		
White collar professional, executive, managerial	16	18
White collar other	22	18
Blue collar	27	29

▼ ▼

Income

Income among the American gay/lesbian population as a whole is slightly lower than that of the heterosexual population. This finding contradicts a popular myth about the relative affluence of American lesbians and gay men, one that is often based on comparisons between general population data and data collected by the sales and marketing departments of gay and lesbian publications, whose readers, by definition, are not representative of the mainstream of all gay consumers.

A more reliable and valid comparison of income is presented in the following tables, using data that compares the general population of gays/lesbians to the general population of heterosexuals. Overall income is slightly lower for the gay/lesbian group as a whole, a difference that is driven primarily by the slightly lower earnings of gay men compared to the heterosexual group.

While it is true that some dual-income, predominantly white, gay male *households* have incomes much greater than the national average, gay males had lower personal and household incomes than their heterosexual counterparts. There is, however, no substantial difference in income distribution between lesbians and heterosexual females; in both cases, female income is below that of males. This observation is especially compelling since discrimination toward women as a group may be more widely spread regardless of race or sexual orientation than previously thought. Certainly much has been written about the economic subjugation of women, but this specific area stands out as one suggesting that more research is warranted.

Lee Badgett's work at the University of Maryland's School of Public Affairs is particularly worth noting here again. Badgett found that gay and bisexual men earn from 9.5 percent to 25.9 percent less than straight men, and that lesbian and bisexual women face a sexual orientation penalty (meaning they fair less well when their "gayness" is known) ranging from 13.1 percent to 14.8, which drops to only 5 percent when taking occupation into account.[11]

▼ ▼

	Gay/Lesbian %	Heterosexual %
PERSONAL INCOME:		
Under $25K	85	78
$25K–$49,999	12	19
$50K–$99,999	2	3
$100K+	1	*
HOUSEHOLD INCOME:		
Under $25K	44	38
$25K–$49,999	39	39
$50K–$99,999	14	20
$100K+	3	3
MEAN PERSONAL INCOME (000)	**$16.9**	**$17.6**
MEAN HOUSEHOLD INCOME (000)	**$35.8**	**$36.7**
MEAN HOUSEHOLD SIZE	**2.89**	**3.01**

*Less than .5%

Income Between the Sexes (Gay/Lesbian and Heterosexual)

	Gay Male %	Heterosexual Male %	Lesbian %	Heterosexual Female %
PERSONAL INCOME:				
Under $25K	81	65	87	88
$25K–$49,999	13	29	11	11
$50K–$99,999	3	5	1	1
$100K+	3	1	*	*
HOUSEHOLD INCOME:				
Under $25K	37	32	47	43
$25K–$49,999	49	42	33	37
$50K–$99,999	9	23	18	17
$100K+	5	3	2	3
MEAN PERSONAL INCOME (000)	**$21.5**	**$22.5**	**$13.3**	**$13.2**
MEAN HOUSEHOLD INCOME (000)	**$37.4**	**$39.3**	**$34.8**	**$34.4**
MEAN HOUSEHOLD SIZE	**3.03**	**3.05**	**2.78**	**2.97**

*Less than 0.5%

SOURCE: Yankelovich MONITOR Gay/Lesbian Perspective

Marital Status

Forty-two percent of the gay/lesbian population report that they are married. While the sex of the spouse is not specified, more than one opinion may often contribute to any given household buying decision. This has significant implications for marketers.

	Gay/Lesbian %	Heterosexual %
CURRENTLY:		
Married	42	54
Never married	44	26

Parental Status

While gay men are less than half as likely as heterosexual males to be fathers, lesbians are nearly as likely to be mothers as their heterosexual counterparts. One-half of the gay/lesbian sample are parents, and one-quarter live in households with children under 18 present. Consequently, there are many products related to parenting that are relevant to this segment of gay/lesbian parents.

	Gay/Lesbian %	Heterosexual %
PARENTS	**50**	**66**
Among women	67	72
Among men	27	60
CHILDREN (UNDER 18) IN HOUSEHOLD		
Among women	32	36
Among men	15	28
MEAN HOUSEHOLD SIZE	**2.89**	**3.01**

Religious Affiliation

Gays/lesbians are less likely to report Protestant religious affiliation. This is especially true of Baptists and may be reflected in the lower representation of this population in the South (where Baptists are more concentrated). There were no other significant differences found in this area.

▼ ▼

	Gay/Lesbian %	Heterosexual %
RELIGIOUS AFFILIATION:		
Protestant (net)	46	56
Baptist	17	27
Churches of Christ	1	3
Disciples of Christ	3	1
Episcopal	6	2
Lutheran	10	6
Methodist	3	8
Presbyterian	2	3
United Church of Christ	1	2
Latter Day Saints/Mormon	*	2
Other Protestant	3	5
Roman Catholic	25	22
Jewish	4	2
Eastern Orthodox	1	1
Unitarian	1	1
Other religion	6	8
None	12	10

*Less than 0.5%

Political Affiliation

In what is sure to be a contoversial and perhaps contested area of fact, the Yankelovich MONITOR data shows what some have long believed but been have unable to confirm—that gay and lesbian Americans are more likely to be Republican than previously thought.

Even within the heterosexual population there has been a widely held belief that the gay/lesbian population is decidedly Democratic, but the data indicate that the gay and lesbian population is no different than its heterosexual counterpart when it comes to the matter of political affiliation. A higher proportion of gays/lesbians do, however, identify themselves as having a liberal political point of view.

▼ ▼

	Gay/Lesbian %	*Heterosexual* %
POLITICAL AFFILIATION:		
Democratic	45	44
Republican	27	26
Independent	21	22
Other	7	8
POLITICAL POINT-OF-VIEW:		
Conservative	34	40
Moderate	37	41
Liberal	28	17
Radical	1	2

Geographic Dispersion by Region

The gay and lesbian population is more likely than the heterosexual population to be found in the north central region of the United States, less likely to be living in the South. Gays/lesbians are more highly concentrated in the top 25 metropolitan counties, and, while there may be concentrations of this population in big coastal cities, its members are relatively widely distributed.

Geography (U.S. Census definitions)	*Gay/Lesbian* %	*Heterosexual* %
NORTHEAST	21	21
New England	3	6
Middle Atlantic	18	15
NORTH CENTRAL	32	23
East North Central	22	17
West North Central	10	6
SOUTH	25	35
South Atlantic	13	18
East South Central	1	6
West South Central	11	11
WEST	22	21
Mountain	4	6
Pacific	18	15

▼ ▼

Geographic Dispersion by Regional Population Size

	Total Population %	Gay/ Lesbian %	Heterosexual %
METROPOLITAN AREA SIZE:			
3 million+	19	27	18
1–3 million	27	34	27
500K–999,999	13	12	14
250K–499,999	10	8	10
100K–249,999	9	5	9
Non-Met area	22	14	21
ONE MILLION OR MORE (NET)	**46**	**61**	**45**
ALL COUNTIES IN 25 LARGEST METROS	**39**	**56**	**38**

Percentage of Self-Identification by Population Size

The following table displays the percentage of gays/lesbians in each metropolitan area according to size. For instance, 8 percent of the population in metropolitan area of 3 million and greater population identify themselves as gay or lesbian.

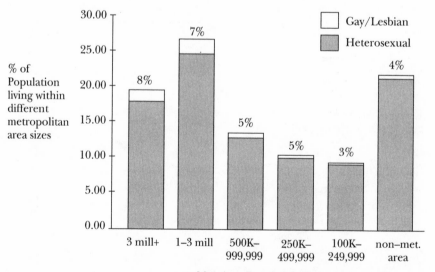

▼ ▼

Attitudinal Profile of Gay and Lesbian Americans

Yankelovich has revealed five key areas of significant difference between the gay/lesbian and the heterosexual populations. Topic areas of difference have been grouped into subjects of significant interest. They are as follows:

- Individuality and self-understanding
- Social interaction
- Experiencing life's diversity
- Maintaining independence
- Skepticism and self-protection

Key Areas of Difference: Individuality and Self-understanding

	Gay/Lesbian %	Heterosexual %
STRONG SUPPORT:		
Personal Regard		
(Need for self-understanding)	43	23
Mind-Body		
(Commitment to maximizing		
health and energy)	44	30
Presence		
(Commitment to maximizing		
physical appearance)	53	42

The gay/lesbian sample appears to be more concerned than the heterosexual population about understanding themselves and their motivations. This is marked by a particularly strong need for self-understanding, which is evident in the data as well as in the interesting notion that many gays/lesbians believe themselves to possess a higher IQ than most, though many feel somewhat alienated from mainstream America. This group's heightened interest in optimizing physical condition and appearance is also clear.

Yankelovich researchers focused further examination of the data in relationship to individual appearance and style and drew the conclusion that there is a stronger interest among gay and lesbian Americans in keeping up with "the latest" in fashion. While this may not be new

▼ ▼

information to many, the heightened interest in physical appearance in combination with other social issues previously discussed draws our attention to issues of self-esteem within the gay and lesbian sample; either less of it, or perhaps a heightened sense of it.

What could be some possible explanations for these interests?

- Increased attention to appearance is a nonverbal communication, affirming gay and lesbian personal good health and strong character
- A need to fit into a perceived standard within a local gay/lesbian community
- A desire to differentiate one's self as separate from or more acceptable to heterosexual society
- As an overcompensating response to a perceived covert plus discrimination by heterosexuals

Key Areas of Difference: Social Interaction and Experiencing Life's Diversity

Companies marketing products that are related to the following list—take note. The gay/lesbian population is clearly and actively looking for new products and services across the board.

	Gay/Lesbian %	Heterosexual %
LOOKING FOR NEW:	%	%
Places to go out with friends	52	42
Foods to eat at home	49	37
Discount stores	30	23
Department stores	29	18
Magazines	26	19
Fast food restaurants	22	15
Home entertainment technology	19	15
Mail order catalogs	15	9

Key Areas of Difference: Maintaining Independence

The data indicate that gays/lesbians perceive a high level of stress in their lives; they appear to feel pressure on all fronts. Only 2

▼ ▼

percent of the sample state that they do not feel that they are under stress (compared to 11 percent of the heterosexual population).

This stress is manifested in a number of buying behaviors, such as a higher level of interest in and consumption of leisure vacations. Sustained feelings of stress appear to lead to a strong need to achieve greater control and certainty in life. Times are not certain and planning for the future is difficult. Frustrated attempts to gain more control become yet another source of stress for this population.

Eighty-five percent of gay males and lesbians feel the need to find ways of reducing stress in their lives. This is a staggeringly high number compared to the heterosexual population. While the ability to remove stress from people's lives may be beyond the scope of marketing, the data indicate an opportunity to add value for the gay/lesbian consumer by streamlining stress out of the product or the purchase decision process.

	Gay/Lesbian	*Heterosexual*
TOTAL AGREE:	%	%
Need to reduce stress in my life	85	78

Key Areas of Difference: Skepticism and Self-protection

The data indicate that gays and lesbians feel less than trusting of their environment—both socially and economically. The following theory was put forth by Yankelovich researcher Rex Briggs to help explain gay and lesbian skepticism and self-protection more precisely.

The Psychology of Disenfranchisement

Three components drive the psychology of disenfranchisement: alienation, cynicism, and perceived victimization. These components interact and intensify each other.

▼ ▼

Alienation

Alienation is one of the most important components of the psychology of disenfranchisement and may be due to negative perceptions, stereotypes, and discrimination condoned and practiced by the dominant culture. The perception of separation from the mainstream culture can create severe stress and can be considered the impetus for the psychology of disenfranchisement.

	Gay/Lesbian %	Heterosexual %
TOTAL AGREE:		
My personal values and point of view are not shared by most Americans today	40	31
Sometimes I have to compromise my principles	76	65
DESCRIBES ME:		
Different from others	55	27
A loner	36	13
Outside the mainstream	24	10

Cynicism

Cynicism is one of the inevitable offshoots of alienation, resulting in the conviction that things will go wrong, that harm is to be expected, and that the only thing that can be trusted is the propensity of bad things to happen. It involves a sense that the "institutions" of society (from which one is alienated) are not only remote, but inimical.

	Gay/Lesbian %	Heterosexual %
TOTAL AGREE:		
With minor exceptions, the honesty and integrity of business in its dealings with the public is at a very high level	37	46
If the opportunity arises, most businesses will take advantage of the public if they feel they are not likely to be found out	63	54

▼ ▼

Victimization

Victimization is a feeling that develops out of the perception of intentional or unintentional undeserved mistreatment by other individuals, organizations, or institutions. Victimization is a logical outgrowth of feelings of cynicism and alienation from the dominant culture.

Communication from Dominant Culture	$\Rightarrow$	Interpretation by Disenfranchised Individual
Malice intended	$\Rightarrow$	Victimization perceived
No malice intended	$\Rightarrow$	Victimization perceived (misinterpreted)
Malice intended	$\Rightarrow$	*No* victimization perceived (misinterpreted)
No malice intended	$\Rightarrow$	*No* victimization perceived

Over time, this cycle can become entrenched. The perceived victimization legitimizes and justifies cynicism in one's mind. The lack of trust fostered by a cynical perspective thereby increases the original feelings of alienation.

The intensity of the feelings of disenfranchisement should be thought of as lying on a continuum stretching from the endpoints of complete enfranchisement to complete disenfranchisement. Few are at either extreme. But all affect the producer-consumer dynamic—especially in relation to gays and lesbians.

ILLUSTRATION: PROCESS IN MOTION

To operationalize this model, imagine two couples—one a gay or lesbian couple and the other a heterosexual couple—waiting for their check in a chaotically busy retaurant.

Communication from Dominant Culture

Both watched as the maitre d' grimaced, perhaps at the thought of having to cram yet another party into the already packed restaurant. Both watched as the waiter took the order of other patrons who appeared to be seated after they were seated. The service was poor, and the waiter rude.

▼ ▼

Interpretation

The heterosexual couple has a tendency to project their dissatisfaction with the service on the inept waiter. The heterosexual couple is likely to attribute the slow service to incompetence on the part of the waiter to adequately deal with the demands of a full restaurant.

The gay or lesbian couple have felt somewhat out of place since the moment they walked in and the maitre d' exchanged what could be interpreted as a rude glance of disapproval after presumably noticing the two of them holding hands. The gay or lesbian couple might interpret the poor service as an intentional or even subconscious slight stemming from homophobia. The disenfranchised gay couple may have entered the restaurant half-expecting to be discriminated against.

Result

While the heterosexual couple may return to try the restaurant again, the gay couple has potentially had their fears of discrimination validated and feel no need to give what they perceive as a homophobic establishment another chance.

Analysis

The poor service provided by the waiter may have been a function of homophobia; on the other hand, it may have been only a function of an understaffed and busy restaurant. However, it is the *interpretation* of the act by the gay or lesbian couple that should be of particular significance to the marketer.

Resulting Needs

The manifestations of the key elements of the psychology of disenfranchisement lead to a number of important needs experienced by the gay/lesbian population that offer the marketer substantial opportunities. They include a need for:

- Self-understanding
  - Recognition of and respect for one's individuality
- Association, a sharing of occasions with "people like me"
- Security (emotional, social, physical)
- Independence

- Stress relief
  - Self-indulgence
  - Escapism

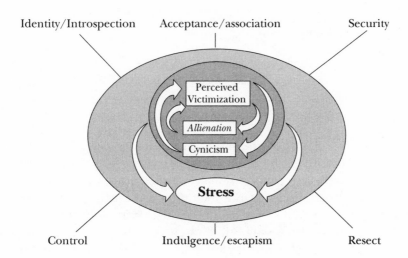

Self-understanding

	Gay/Lesbian %	Heterosexual %
TOTAL AGREE:		
Concerned about self-understanding	57	41
Feel the need for self-reflection	80	68
Feel the need to explore my sense of spirituality	71	62

Association

There appears to be a need to build and maintain allegiances with "people like me." This group not only has a need to associate with those who share the same sexual orientation, but also needs to associate with similar ethnic backgrounds. This group may respond to marketers that embrace diversity along a number of dimensions (sexual orientation, gender, ethnic, socioeconomic, etc.).

▼ ▼

	Gay/Lesbian %	Heterosexual %
TOTAL AGREE:		
I feel I must maintain some sort of allegiance to people with similar ethnic roots to my own	57	46

Security

This population has been the target of both hate and physical violence because of its sexual orientation; it is thus not surprising that gays/lesbians are concerned about their personal safety. This has ramifications not only for a number of products that have direct application to personal safety (home security systems and the like), but also for those with less tangible safety features such as a photograph on the front of a credit card that is intended to protect the card holder. This is yet another area where marketers can transform product attributes into consumer benefits by linking such features to the needs of the gay/lesbian consumer.

	Gay/Lesbian %	Heterosexual %
ACTIVITIES LIMITED OR AVOIDED BECAUSE OF THE FEAR OF CRIME:		
Walking at night	56	52
Carrying more cash than is actually needed	50	41
Allowing sales people into the home	47	32
Going to an ATM at night	32	25
Going into the city	26	18
Riding public transportation	25	21
Having home delivery of newspapers	16	14
Carry credit cards	15	12

▼ ▼

Independence

The data clearly points to an increased need to "stand alone."

	Gay/Lesbian %	Heterosexual %
TOTAL AGREE:		
Lately I find I'm looking for ways to create more independence in my life	83	72

Stress Relief

As noted earlier, gays/lesbians report substantially higher levels of stress than the heterosexual population, and that stress comes from a broad variety of sources. Money, jobs, personal and family relationships are all sources of concern. Health, which was not included in the questionnaire item listing sources of stress, would certainly be an important contributor to stress for many in the era of AIDS. Reducing stress is of paramount importance to this population, an area where marketers can help in both practical and emotional terms.

	Gay/Lesbian %	Heterosexual %
CAUSING MORE STRESS THAN LAST YEAR:		
Money Concerns	73	57
Work/job	61	40
Personal life	58	38
Planning for the future	51	49
Parents	28	18
Other	30	25
Not under stress	2	11

Self-Indulgence/Escapism

Forty-two percent of gay males and lesbians feel the need (either strongly or moderately) to take something to calm their nerves.

▼ ▼

Tranquilizers and sleeping pill usage is significantly higher among the gay/lesbian sample. Nearly 40 percent of gay males agree that it is becoming more difficult to find peace and quiet in their lives. Over 50 percent of gay males agree that home is the only place they can really relax and unwind. These numbers indicate the need, especially among gay men, to find immediate solutions to the overwhelming stress and anxiety each experiences on a daily basis.

Products that emphasize the comfort of home, or help to create a tranquil environment, may have a market with gay males and lesbians.

	Gay/Lesbian %	Heterosexual %
TOTAL AGREE:		
I like to imagine myself doing something I know I wouldn't dare do	62	48
Feel the need to take something to calm my nerves	42	27
Sometimes I feel that my home is the only place I can really relax and unwind	42	32
It's becoming more and more difficult to find peace and quiet in my life	32	23

Business and Marketing Implications

Communications that focus on serving any of the aforementioned needs are likely to strike a chord with the gay male or lesbian consumer and encourage a purchase or a more favorable corporate image among gay and lesbian consumers. Business and marketers can offset the negative effects of the cycle of disenfranchisement and build a valuable relationship in several ways:

- Develop, print, and circulate an employment hiring policy prohibiting discrimination based on sexual orientation in all areas of the workplace.

▼ ▼

- Communicate this information in press releases to gay and lesbian organizations and publications.
- Investigate initiating domestic partnership benefits for gay and lesbian employees, or supplement employee compensation packages to gay and lesbian employees in a way that uniformly parallels the insurance benefits enjoyed by heterosexual employees.
- Encourage and give management support to gay and lesbian employee groups in the workplace.
- Focus on inclusion of gays/lesbians in the consumer family (offsets alienation).
- Identify cultural reference points to which gays/lesbians can relate. Avoid stereotypes.
- Develop honest and consistent messages related to product offerings (to minimize cynicism).
- Under-promise and over-deliver (to minimize victimization).
- Communicate respect for the consumer.
- When something does go wrong, do more than just fix it (defuses cynicism, relieves feelings of victimization).
- It is imperative to listen patiently and attentively to complaints.
- Accept blame.
- Fix the problem.
- Provide additional compensation.
- Reduce stress.
- Streamline stress out of the purchase process.
- Offer opportunities for healthy self-indulgence.

The overriding point for business leaders as well as marketers and employee managers, however, is that many gay males and lesbians view the world through a prism of cynicism toward business, are quick to interpret actions as attempts at victimization, and feel alienated from the dominant culture. Marketing and employee communication strategies that take into consideration the influence of these factors can sidestep the pitfalls and leverage the benefits of their management approaches and product or service offerings, and thus increase the success of their business, management, and consumer marketing planning.

▼ ▼

And, as has been established in many industries and consumer market segments, genuinely seeking to accommodate gays/lesbians in the workplace and the marketplace positions a company as being "more socially conscious," thereby buttressing brand loyalty among heterosexual consumers as well.

▼ ▼

CHAPTER 5

BRAND LOYALTY, MANAGEMENT, AND THE CREATIVE PROCESS

Promoting Products and Services to Gay and Lesbian Consumers

You can't fake a Corporate Soul; either you have one or you'd better create one, fast.

FAITH POPCORN[1]

In the best of all possible worlds, the following criteria would place any company wishing to target gay and lesbian consumers in a good competitive position:

- A stated policy of nondiscrimination based on sexual orientation in hiring, promotion, and workplace ethics.
- Employee benefits company-wide that provide gay and lesbian workers with the same level of health care, bereavement leave, sick leave, and other benefits that are extended to heterosexual workers. In other words, domestic partnership benefits that apply to the designated partner or significant other of the gay or lesbian employee, administered in a fashion equal to those that are made available to legally married partners of heterosexual employees.

▼ ▼

- An official, comprehensive sensitivity training program for all employees that includes information about social diversity with regard to race, ethnicity, and sexual orientation. Ideally, that program would include information about HIV prevention, AIDS education, and specifically, information of special concern to women and women's health.
- A gay and lesbian employees group that is acknowledged and officially supported from the highest level of the company.
- A high-profile supporter of at least one gay/lesbian–oriented or civil rights–oriented philanthropic organization.
- No corporate history of supporting or making in-kind contributions to political action committees or organizations among whose goals are the reinstatement of state sodomy laws or passage of ordinances to prevent gay and lesbian Americans from obtaining equal status or protection under the law at municipal, state, or federal level.

Of course, not all companies in America are large enough, progressive enough, or in strong enough financial positions that would allow them to install all the above policies company-wide. Domestic partnership benefits for gay and lesbian Americans are particularly challenging to administer in large corporations where benefit packages have to be provided across state lines or different divisions within a company.

For this reason, I believe that it is unreasonable for gay and lesbian consumers to judge the companies they do business with based on whether or not a company has domestic partnership benefits for its gay and lesbian employees. But other issues, particularly those related to nondiscrimination policies and support of gay and lesbian philanthropy (or a visible organization that supports gay and lesbian equality such as the American Civil Liberties Union) should be fundamental to a company's long-term relationship with gay and lesbian consumers.

First Things First

Listed below are the most important guidelines to consider before launching any marketing program that seeks to communicate a message to gay and lesbian consumers (these should be considered even by companies that do not currently intend to target gays and

▼ ▼

lesbians as a niche market). Although some suggestions may, upon first glance, appear to be basic common sense rules, they are routinely overlooked by many American businesses.

These guidelines can apply to any businessperson or company wishing to position products in the mainstream consumer print and electronic media or in association with gay/lesbian-focused media. Both channels can certainly provide solid forays into the places where gay and lesbian consumers make purchasing decisions. Ideally, however, most companies will want to target gay and lesbian consumers through both the national and regional marketplace.

Besides these recommendations to executives and entrepreneurs, the decision-making process regarding gay and lesbian issues in business should be taken up at every level where gay and lesbian individuals are likely to be engaged. The goals of positioning the company's business in relation to product placement and advertising should be made at the marketing level. Marketers must decide for themselves and their company what media and what approach is best suited for a given product or service in a given industry. However, for marketers, considerations must still be made in four immediate domains of particular importance:[2]

Corporate Policy

At minimum, a company conducting business with gay and lesbian consumers must have a nondiscrimination policy statement. For some companies, all that is required is the simple insertion of two words, *sexual* and *orientation*, into the existing policy. A company's legal counsel should be consulted regarding the addition of these words and the grandfathering of a nondiscriminatory policy company-wide.

If your company does not have a policy, immediately establish one or begin lobbying the right people to get one installed. Companies that target gay and lesbian consumers without having first taken this step leave themselves and their employees vulnerable to a multitude of harassment lawsuits and potential public relations challenges down the road.

In its best form, a corporate policy statement should include language preventing discrimination against people with HIV and AIDS; a statement that the company's support for gay and lesbian employee groups is tantamount to those of heterosexuals; diversity

▼ ▼

training that includes sexual orientation discussions; and some kind of domestic partnership benefits compensation package for gay and lesbian employees that is equal to those enjoyed by married heterosexual employees.

Corporate Action

Publicly back up the corporate policy of not discriminating based on sexual orientation by supporting or contributing in-kind services to organizations that defend gay and lesbian individuality.

Every city in the United States with a population of 250,000 or more has some kind of gay or lesbian organization or is within driving distance of a larger city that does. Marketers and the companies they serve cannot afford to be perceived by a single gay or lesbian consumer as exploitive or on a mission to "profit off of them." Besides, too many companies sooner or later find themselves in a position where they have to take a stand on some community, industry, or political issue of importance to their customers. It pays to be—and to have been all along—on the official side of a company's customers.

In addition, gay and lesbian organizations support and bring vitality to urban markets across the United States and are always looking for support from local area businesses in return. Indeed, local gay and lesbian organizations provide one of the easiest ways for a company to politically align itself with the community—the very people with whom it is seeking to do business.

Clarence Patton, program coordinator with Empire State Pride Agenda, a gay and lesbian political action committee in New York, sees gay and lesbian organizations as the principal watchdogs who are "creating visibility; their mission is to improve the quality of life of lesbian and gay people."

Paula Ettelbrick, legislative counsel for Empire State Pride Agenda agrees, stating, "When we are invisible, our very existence can be denied." Marketers across America need to understand this constant—that despite different areas of focus in helping gay and lesbian emancipation, nearly every gay and lesbian organization in the United States is ultimately fighting for the same thing in their lobbying and activism efforts for equal rights and protection under the law: visibility and a better quality of life for all gay and lesbian Americans. Business cannot go wrong by getting behind these regional and national efforts.

A pioneering example of same-sex imagery that communicates a sense of warmth and "matter-of-factness" about a new product of particular interest to gay male consumers.

Carefully produced and strategically placed Marlboro billboards have long appeared in neighborhoods across America where gay as well as straight consumers will easily notice their presence.

taking a break
is who you
take it with."

VIRGINIA SLIMS
YOU'VE COME A
LONG WAY BABY

SURGEON GENERAL'S WARNING: Quitting Smoking
Greatly Reduces Serious Risks to Your Health

A strong advertising communication that speaks to many different demographic groups of women, regardless of income, race, or sexual orientation.

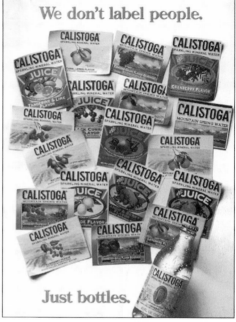

We don't label people.

Just bottles.

This shows how a company can position a product to gay and lesbian consumers while also communicating inclusiveness to all consumer groups. It's clean, brand-focused, and matter-of-fact.

Whimsical, unoffending production design communicates many different things to many different groups of men, especially the importance of having a sense of individuality.

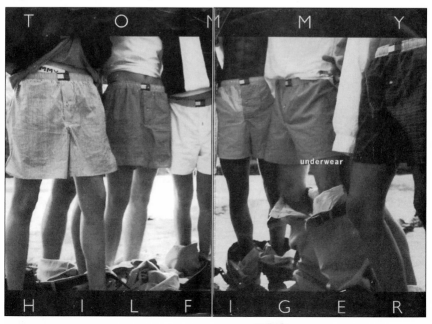

TOMMY

underwear

HILFIGER

A strong state-of-the-art example of well-crafted advertising that communicates same-sex attraction and a sense of realness about gay male culture. Everything is on cue, from the wardrobe choice to the game being played.

Benetton has mastered the art of communicating diversity to a broad range of consumers on a broad range of social issues. Everything has been tackled, from war and the environment to HIV, condom use, American democracy, and the politics of sexual identity.

Placing Martina Navratilova next to wide receiver Art Monk is brilliant because it directly communicates diversity across a broad consumer demographic spectrum: sports enthusiasts (whether they are men or women), racial minorities, and gay as well as straight consumers.

Great target marketing on behalf of AT&T. A well-utilized play on the use of the word *true* as a pun that serves to communicate inclusiveness in many different ways while also educating the consumer about the product's benefits.

There's one Travelers Cheque for couples who don't always sightsee eye to eye.

Focusing on just how versatile American Express Travelers Cheques really are serves as a way to position not only the product but the entire company as inclusive, contemporary, and innovative. This ad appeared in *Out* magazine; note the two female signatories.

This leading commercial was a first in television advertising. It communicated inclusiveness across a broad range of consumer groups while allowing gay men to be seen as everyday people. If IKEA's next commercial includes lesbians, their competitors will really have their work cut out for them.

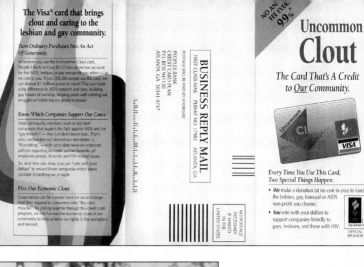

Companies that provide exclusive products to gay men and lesbians and then follow up by sharing some of their profits with the gay community will always be seen as the leaders.

Gay and lesbian consumers will always appreciate the witty and the sassy. Dewar's has clearly found a way to tease everyone by intimating what is usually forbidden discussion among polite company.

Spectacular representation of dual messaging to straight and gay men. It communicates a clear and believable sense of company friendliness and trustworthiness.

The beach "kiss" has been the mainstay of heterosexual advertisements since the 1950s and is now re-created by Olivia in this new benchmark of lesbian consumer marketing.

By playing on a theme from the American war years, Diesel has formulated for gay men the same iconography that Olivia has developed for lesbians.

Since the early ACT-UP years, Miller Beer has become a visible part of the national gay and lesbian advertising community's support network—both in their treatment of marketing campaigns and in their support of nonprofit fundraising.

The magazine known for communicating a cutting-edge sense of glamour attained new heights of respectability with gay and lesbian consumers by producing this very witty, tongue-in-cheek cover that got lots of attention in the media and in many different social circles.

There was a time when the *New Yorker* would not have acknowledged this level of versimilitude (or even satire) when it comes to gay visibility. The magazine has clearly incorporated an understanding of the gay and lesbian consumer since Tina Brown's installation as editor in chief, and her lead in making more editorial space for gay-and-lesbian-themed articles has been well received.

Mainstream America first began to accept the truth about AIDS and the importance of gay and lesbian culture in the early 1980s. However, noticeable advertising and editorial imagery—both about and aimed at gay and lesbian consumers on a regular basis—did not begin to appear widely in the national media until the 1990s.

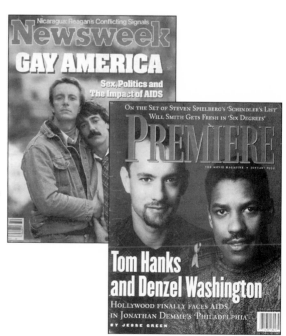

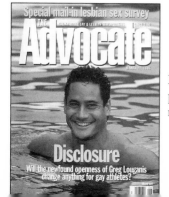

Being gay, HIV positive, and a celebrity is now part of mainstream American advertising and media imagery.

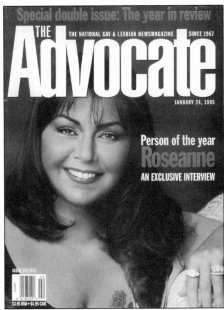

There was a time when some gay and lesbian consumers would have been insulted by the appearance of mainstream celebrities on gay magazine covers. Times and attitudes have clearly changed as magazines and celebrities—both gay and straight—now seek each other out in an effort to communicate their understanding of both diversity and gay and lesbian culture while also positioning themselves to appeal to a rapidly changing consumer marketplace.

▼ ▼

Almost any company in America that seeks to support the simple, fundamental values that are of concern to local or national gay and lesbian organizations—that of visibility and equal protection under the law—will have succeeded in jumping the most important hurdle in the race to develop brand loyalty and a smooth public relationship with these consumers.

Market Research

Conducting extensive research prior to the launch of any advertising campaign aimed at gay and lesbian consumers is elementary marketing logic. Many marketers have no idea what demographics of, or what exact segment within, the overall gay and lesbian market spectrum they hope to reach. Is your company intending to target men and women? What age group? What income category?

Treat the research process with the same level of sophistication, importance, and budget allowances as any other market research project within the company.

Produce testing campaigns and run focus groups comprised of gay and lesbian and heterosexual participants. Ideally, focus groups with gay and lesbian consumers should be conducted by gay or lesbian moderators who make their own sexual orientation known to the participants.

If the budget allows, marketing materials intended to attract gay and lesbian consumers should also be cross-tested against focus groups comprised exclusively of heterosexuals. It is important to gauge how the bulk of a company's current consumers might react to a gay/lesbian-specific targeted campaign and visa versa.

Focus groups comprised exclusively of gay and lesbian participants always yield surprising and useful insights that can be applied to an entire range of concerns within a company's marketing strategy. Research, research, research—it pays. Allocate money to gay and lesbian focus groups or market testing. Companies serious about targeting gay and lesbian consumers cannot afford not to.

Community Involvement

For smaller companies, this is a particularly important area. One of the easiest ways to go about launching a gay/lesbian-oriented advertising campaign in small to mid-size cities is to consult with a company's current gay and lesbian employees or with the gay and lesbian business community in a given company's principal area of

▼ ▼ ▼ ▼ ▼ ▼ ▼ ▼ ▼ ▼ ▼ ▼ ▼ ▼ ▼ ▼ ▼ ▼ ▼ ▼

economic activity. Some of the best marketing ideas and concepts come from gay and lesbian clergy, civic representatives and volunteers, the assembly line, administrative support staffs, traffic departments, and proofreading pools.

Communicate the decision to target gay and lesbian consumers to managers and supervisors and encourage them to utilize interested employees by allowing them to attend brainstorming sessions for creative development of campaigns. The results are always surprising and the degree of goodwill fostered within a company's labor force is immeasurable.

Moreover, every major American city now has writers, art directors, and in some cases entire advertising agencies that specialize in gay/lesbian-oriented marketing and research. Even in America's smaller cities, a business can always turn to the advertising department of a local gay and lesbian newspaper and usually obtain competent and cost-effective advertising and marketing advice.

But the point still stands—for both large and small companies—conduct research first; facts always matter.

Competent and shrewd marketers seeking to target gay and lesbian consumers in American business regularly utilize, customize, and combine these four areas of focus (corporate policy, corporate action, market research, and community involvement) with existing knowledge about the company's products and services.

The end result is always a cunning and powerful advertising campaign that wins gay and lesbian customers and instills broad-scale goodwill within a company. Be resourceful, be inclusive. It will be apparent in the marketing campaign and the results.

Take Action, Be Decisive

Once the four areas above have been made part of the process, it is critical for the marketer, advertiser, or business owner to be aggressive about implementing the plans as soon as possible.

Gay and lesbian consumers can be extremely skeptical. They also have extremely well-calibrated cow pie detectors. A campaign that has had too many hands in it for too long will always come off looking contrived, hollow, forced, too clean, or simply dull. Expect the very nature of the subject to provoke discussion and debate within a company and within the press. Campaigns that are good generate lots of press—positive press, which translates to free advertising (IKEA's campaign is particularly true in this case as is Greg Louganis's book and Melissa Etheridge's music). In addition, debate and discussion are healthy. But opinions are like beautiful eyes, everyone has at least two. Each person brings his or her own insights, prejudices, and insecurities into every decision-making process—but the benefits of confronting creative issues surrounding sexual orientation are well worth any temporary nervousness about openness. The key, though, is to be decisive, because as with markets, openness breeds competition, fuels ingenuity, and leads to growth. But not if marketing and business leaders vacillate.

As the competition heats up for gay and lesbian customers in thousands of different product and service industries across the United States, profits will begin shifting between companies, between brands, and even among stockholders. And in the coming months ahead, for the business leaders who do not heed the warning signs being raised by the gay and lesbian consumer revolution in America, there stands the distinct possibility of encountering a road riddled with political, brand positioning, and public relations nightmares.

Corporate Nightmares: The Truth About Boycotts and Backlash

The gay and lesbian community cannot be bought. Nor can it be repressed, silenced, or shoved back into the closet by right-wing extremists. It can, however, be earned, marketed to, and invested in by sound business and marketing practices.

There's always been talk about backlash when it comes to gay and lesbian marketing. Fortunately for business and for gay and lesbian consumerism, there is more talk than example.

The most costly backlashes have come from within the gay and lesbian community—usually brought on by companies that have not maintained a decent relationship with them as consumers or American citizens—not from Christian fundamentalists refusing to buy a brand of detergent because a prime-time television show introduced a gay character.

There are some cases, however. One was when numerous sponsors refused to advertise on an early 1990s episode of *Thirtysomething* that portrayed two gay male characters having a conversation in bed.

▼ ▼

Unfortunately for the fundamentalists, that news issue came and went in about a week. Since that time, numerous gay and lesbian characters have been introduced on television sitcoms and feature dramas during prime-time viewing hours with no backlash. Roseanne's famous "lesbian kiss" episode actually increased ratings and market share, as did the Barbra Streisand NBC production starring Glenn Close as Margarethe Cammermeyer, the true story about a gay woman who was discharged from the U.S. military.

Boycotts perhaps became the most popular during the 1960s when various groups began picketing and raising public attention about companies that were supplying materials for the U.S. military during the Vietnam War. It was at this time that "the phenomenon of socially responsible investing probably originated," writes Ed Mickens in *The Advocate*.[3] Mickens further comments that in the 1970s stockholder actions and boycotts "became popular as a way to put the economic squeeze on the apartheid government of South Africa. . . . The tactic or its threat worked, at least in the sense that most American companies withdrew from South Africa."

This kind of shareholder action was somewhat duplicated in the gay and lesbian community in their attempt to drive the Cracker Barrel Old Country Store, Inc., to reconsider its antigay position on hiring gay and lesbian employees. In 1991 the company fired at least eleven employees, allegedly because they were gay or were thought to be gay or lesbian.

The first shareholder resolution against Cracker Barrel was in April of 1994 and was sponsored by the New York City Comptroller's office. It sought the reinstating of fired gay and lesbian employees and recommended the adoption of a nondiscrimination policy based on sexual orientation. It garnered over 15 percent of the vote among shareholders of Cracker Barrell stock in 1994 and about the same again in 1995, according to Dianne Bratcher, co-chair of the Wall Street Project (an organization of gay and lesbian shareholder activists) that helped lead the fight. To date the action has not yet resulted in the changing of Cracker Barrel's management policy, but its stock, which grew enormously between 1988 and 1992 has remained largely unchanged since Cracker Barrel's troubles with gay and lesbian consumers began.

Recently the Wall Street Project compiled and released its Equality Principles on Sexual Orientation, a voluntary code of con-

▼ ▼

duce that aims to achieve equality in the workplace (see this chap-ter's endnotes). According to the press release dated May 4, 1995, and endoresed by Barney Frank and Gerry Studds (U.S. congress-men from Massachusetts) and New York City Comptroller Allan Hevisi:

> The eight principles outline how the leaders of the Wall Street Project believe lesbians, gay men, and bisexuals want to be treated in the workplace and marketplace. Similar inititatives, the Sullivan Principles on South Africa, the MacBride Principles on Fair Employment in Northern Ireland, and the Ceres Principles on the Environment, have established shareholder activism as a viable tool in creating social change.

As gay and lesbian consumers continue to organize and make their concerns known not only to government but to Wall Street, the real backlash threat that marketers and stockholders need to be aware of is the one that can erupt from within the gay and lesbian community itself.

One of the most memorable gay and lesbian boycotts in American history was launched against the Florida Citrus Commission in 1977. It lasted over two years and was motivated directly by Anita Bryant's Save Our Children campaign, which had placed full-page advertise-ments in the *Miami Herald* claiming that "the recruitment of our chil-dren is absolutely necessary for the survival and growth of homosexu-ality." The advertisment went on to say, "Since homosexuals cannot reproduce, they must recruit, must freshen the ranks. Cultures throughout history have dealt with homosexuals almost universally with disdain, abhorrence, disgust—even death."

The boycott led to Anita Bryant's contract not being renewed by the commission and her singing career suffering a permanent set-back as well. Looking back, many now consider her campaign against gay and lesbian Americans as unnecessarily obsessive and bizarre. But Ms. Bryant's campaign was more in reaction to the flex-ing of gay and lesbian activist muscle at the municipal level. She had specifically embarked on a mission to repeal Dade County's gay and lesbian equal protection clause and ended up dragging the orange juice industry along with her.

While it cannot be proven that orange juice sales suffered any great slump because of the boycott, the Florida Citrus Commission was placed in the position of dealing with a national public relations nightmare, which has still not been forgotten by many gay and lesbian—as well as heterosexual—consumers.

Another memorable corporate nightmare launched with the help of gay and lesbian consumers involves Coors Beer.

Adolph Coors Company in Golden, Colorado, has attempted to target the gay and lesbian consumer ever since a boycott of their company erupted and gained national attention in the late 1970s. The accusations then were many, most specifically that the company had allegedly engaged in union busting and had given lie detector tests to individuals seeking employment—allegedly including questions about sexual orientation—and that Coors had contributed money to Anita Bryant's anti-gay crusade.

A boycott was urged from within various corridors of the gay and lesbian community and an official one was launched on April 12, 1977, by the AFL-CIO in support of Brewery Workers (Local 366) which was not rescinded until 1987. Coors denied all the accusations, yet finding itself under such public pressure, was forced to begin moving swiftly in the public relations arena. Shortly after the boycott was called, Joe Coors himself was quoted in *The Nation* as saying, "I honestly see very little appropriate role for unions in this day and age," which arguably made matters worse.[4]

Since that time, the company's public image has been changed somewhat through an ongoing marketing and public relations effort that has included the placement of advertisements in the gay and lesbian press as well as sponsorship of gay and lesbian community events. But their past will always follow them in the eyes of older gay and lesbian consumers, who will never forget.

As Russ Bellant wrote in *The Coors Connection: How Coors Family Philanthropy Undermines Democratic Pluralism,* "A number of affidavits, sworn testimony before the Senate, and press reports indicate that Coors did indeed use the polygraph to impose its narrow political views and quest for sexual conformity upon workers."[5] In its associations with right-wing political groups, Coors tries to impose those same views on the entire public.[6]

Since the early 1980s, Coors (the company) has contributed hundreds of thousands of dollars to various gay, lesbian, and AIDS groups. But the Coors family has also contributed hundreds of thousands of dollars to political action groups and committees that seek to deny gays and lesbians their civil rights. Although there have been changes both in Coors' management and marketing decision-making regarding gay and lesbian consumers, the majority of the company stock—which includes the Zima brand alcoholic beverage—is still held by the Coors family, a fact that is widely known among gay and lesbian consumers. So is the fact that the Coors family has supported conservative organizations like the Heritage Foundation and the Free Congress Foundation—both of which have routinely espoused public policies that would essentially deny gay and lesbian Americans their right to privacy and equal protection under the law if enacted.

Coors really has no choice but to continue its public relations and marketing campaign aimed at gay and lesbian consumers if for no other reason than to protect its reputation among non–gay and lesbian consumers. Indeed, it's hard to argue to the unknowing person on the street that Coors is a "homophobic company" if Coors and Zima advertising routinely shows up in gay and lesbian publications and on the side of floats in gay and lesbian pride parades.

This buying of advertising space in the gay and lesbian community may actually be money that is being spent to buttress brand loyalty and identity among gay and lesbian consumers not old enough to know the history—and therein lies the next generation of Coors (and Zima) drinkers—and Coors must know that.

In 1990, a similar challenge was presented to Philip Morris in relationship to its Miller beer and Marlboro cigarette brands.

The company had been making contributions to Senator Jesse Helms, one of America's most outspoken anti-gay and anti-lesbian political leaders. Helms's position on AIDS research funding and prevention ideology was and continues to be unbelievably inhumane and counter to the goals not only of people living with HIV and AIDS, but the vast majority of gay and lesbian Americans, their families, and friends.

When information regarding the sheer size of the contributions Philip Morris was making to Jesse Helms got out, AIDS activists (namely ACT-UP) launched a high-profile, relatively successful 1990 boycott of Miller beer to "protest parent company Philip Morris's contributions to the hatemonger Senator Jesse Helms." The cover of the August issue of *Outweek* magazine illustrated Jesse Helms dressed in drag as the Wicked Witch of the West (wearing Dorothy's ruby red slippers) riding on a bottle of Miller and smoking a Marlboro with the headline "Surrender Jesse!"

▼ ▼

In the end, Philip Morris did not stop funding Helms but did agree to increase its funding to AIDS-related research (nearly doubling its contributions—already over a million dollars), which resulted in the boycott being called off by ACT-UP.

Some older lesbians and gay men will still not drink Miller beer. Other boycotts and public demonstrations against major companies have received widespread attention, including those aimed at Burroughs Wellcome for what was seen by many as price-gouging of AZT medication for Americans living with HIV and AIDS and the state of Colorado for attempted passage of Amendment 2, a law barring measures that protect lesbians and gay men against discrimination. At least seven Colorado municipalities have passed such measures. The law has been appealed to the Supreme Court.

Forewarned Is Forearmed

Your company or the one you work for can learn from the mistakes of Coors, Philip Morris, Cracker Barrel, and the state of Colorado. Corporate policy and corporate action in relationship to gay and lesbian consumers do in fact matter in modern America. And gay and lesbian consumers have made it clear that they are willing to boycott, conduct public demonstrations, and are adept at gaining pubic support for their grievances.

With each passing year, more and more mainstream companies rush to support the gay and lesbian community during America's annual gay pride and freedom day celebrations held each June. And each year, the political pressure on legislators increases as the press and electronic media present more accurate images of gay and lesbian Americans as they really are.

Each year the stakes get higher in the fight for equal rights for gays and lesbians. And each year gay and lesbian visibility grows, another gay-themed movie gets released, another lesbian kiss makes its way onto prime-time television.

The issues related to gay and lesbian visibility—equal rights, equal protection under the law, and gay and lesbian market muscle—are not going to go away. There will eventually be a federal statute barring discrimination against gay and lesbian individuals in housing, employment, and healthcare across the United States.

There is no sound reason for America's companies to not plan on getting on board with these issues ahead of time. It simply makes good marketing sense. It's also the right thing to do. CEOs, presidents, vice-presidents, senior-level managers, and public relations directors need to look at the companies they're working in and ask themselves if they can really afford to have one of their brands seriously boycotted, debated, or dragged through the national press by gay and lesbian political leaders, AIDS activists, labor groups, and other human rights organizations.

The answer is no. It is never in the best interest of business to have to fight a boycott or negative press, particularly in relation to domestic human rights issues. And as proven by the hits taken by the companies mentioned above—it is also exceedingly costly.

Good News

The good news is that American business is already selling hundreds of millions of dollars' worth of products and services to gay and lesbian consumers each year, through thousands of different industries. And the companies that are doing the most business with gay and lesbian consumers are—not surprisingly—the companies that have the strongest reputations among gay and lesbian individuals as a group. Most of them got their reputations by subscribing to the ethics and policies described earlier in this chapter.

In short, good companies maintain good corporate policies. Smart companies hoping to attract gay and lesbian consumers also make use of an age-old medical axiom that they add to their sound corporate policies: An ounce of prevention is worth a pound of cure.

This is a simple piece of advice that every American company should take now regarding gay and lesbian marketing. But it should not be viewed as some half-baked public relations stopgap measure. It is a philosophy—a corporate attitude and moral outlook in relationship to business.

Customers run your business. And the simple fact is that much of America's retail customers are gay and lesbian whether America's companies know it or not.

As consciousness about gay and lesbian consumerism becomes more apparent in American business, so will each individual company's realizations about its own percentage (or potential percentage) of gay and lesbian customers and employees. And when

▼ ▼

it comes to gay and lesbian employees and gay and lesbian consumers, the two often go hand in hand at the corporate level. A
good barometer of these developments can be found in the development of gay and lesbian employee groups that are cropping up
at major corporations around the country (one of the most visible
of these can be found at AT&T, called LEAGUE (Lesbians,
Bisexual and Gay United Employees).

The companies that refuse to address gay and lesbian employee-
and consumer-related issues do so at their eventual peril—both in
their ability to attract a talented and vibrant work force and in
their eventual capacity to compete for what will soon prove to be
required marketing in all kinds of product and service industries.

Listening to Leaders

What follows here is a loose-knit series of excerpts and discussions
with various individuals who have shared their insights in relationship to gay and lesbian social and economic issues. It is my intention that by sharing portions of these conversations verbatim that
the reader can begin to grasp a level of sensibility about gay and lesbian marketing culture and its relationship to social visibility, AIDS,
politics, and the general mix of media.

By gaining insights into how gay and lesbian culture is being
infused into the imagery and lexicon of mainstream communication, marketers can begin to develop their own insights and strategies for increased sales and heightened brand loyalty among gay
and lesbian consumers. Developing a competitive edge in this marketplace requires more than corporate willingness; it requires segmentation, targeting, strategizing, and seeking out important new
niches within the gay and lesbian market spectrum. In other words,
building customer alliances.

New Relationships

Gaining and keeping gay and lesbian consumers, like heterosexual
consumers, is about relationship building. But in the coming years,
the development of that relationship needs to be built on much
more solid ground with gay and lesbian consumers than has been
traditionally necessary with heterosexual consumers. If American
companies want to attract and keep gay and lesbian consumers,

then they have to learn to talk to those consumers on a variety of commercial terrains above and beyond where the consumers are doing the majority of their spending.

That begins inside the doors of the company.

Ed Mickens stated at the very beginning of his book, *The 100 Best Companies for Gay Men and Lesbians* (Pocket Books 1994):

> Employers who do well addressing gay and lesbian issues are the organizations that will excel in the years to come. They will probably outshine their competitors. They will grow and develop profitably in their industries. They will find creative new ways to flourish in the uncertain marketplace of the 1990s and likely the new millennium beyond.
>
> Why?
>
> Talent. Plus openness and an ability to change.
>
> This doesn't mean that companies will excel *only* because they are good with lesbian and gay issues. But it is a revealing indicator. Organizations that address gay and lesbian issues demonstrate a willingness to listen and respond to the concerns of their employees. All their employees.

This fact is also echoed in *Cracking the Corporate Closet*, where authors Sean Strub, Dan Baker, and Bill Henning state:

> The most basic measure of how an American corporation stands on treating its lesbian and gay employees as equals is whether or not it has an anti-discrimination policy or equal employment opportunity statement that includes the term "sexual orientation" or "sexual preference."

Even though it has been stated previously, it's really that simple. Marketers interested in targeting gay and lesbian consumers must first investigate their companies' own stated policies regarding this issue. They must understand that that commitment must precede any conspicuously launched advertising campaign in the marketplace that may result in press attention or awaken discussions in the political arena. A company needs to be able to point to its corporate policy statement and record.

General Motors knows this. So does General Electric, RJR Nabisco, Procter & Gamble, AT&T, Apple Computers, Levi Strauss, Harley Davidson, IBM, Eastman Kodak, and Ben & Jerry's. These leading

▼ ▼

companies and hundreds of others have moved to position themselves in a way that is satisfactory to their employees as well as the
future of their business.[7]

The remarks below that I recorded in an interview with Linda
Workman, who was hired in February of 1991 as director of Work
Force Diversity at RJR Nabisco, typify the leading philosophy that is
inspiring change in business—particularly about diversity in hiring
and workplace ethics for both large and small businesses across
America:

> At RJR Nabisco, the way in which we approach diversity is to be all-inclusive.
> Companies that are responsive and sensitive to diversity issues are the compa-
> nies that are going to have the advantage in the marketplace, which is why my
> position was created in 1991. I was hired at a time when our corporate cul-
> ture was changing. The commitment to change came from the top of the orga-
> nization, from our chairman and CEO at the time.

According to Ms. Workman, the move toward more, not less,
inclusion, acceptance, and incorporation of the values and attitudes of a changing work force is about to sweep American business:

> [The] government-sponsored report published by the Hudson Institute, the
> Workforce 2000 report, basically said that American business should prepare
> for some major demographic changes in the work force by the year 2000. We
> can expect to see very large numbers of women and people of color and a
> declining proportion of white males. It will be a big enough change that com-
> panies are going to have to learn how to manage this diversity. By the year
> 2000, 85 percent of new entrants will be women, minorities, or immigrants;
> that's a pretty remarkable statistic. . . . The bottom line of the report is that
> America's future work force will be very diverse.

Regarding sexual and racial politics and issues and what their
effects can mean in the corporate environment, Ms. Workman continued:

> Women and people of color will not be satisfied not to advance, and the gay
> and lesbian community has made it clear that they are unwilling to be second-
> class citizens. They've been successful at putting their issues forward in
> Congress and in business. The repeated visibility and emphasis that the gay
> and lesbian community has been persistent in presenting has certainly caused
> corporations to listen more closely.

▼ ▼

Companies that have taken as broad a view of diversity, as we have, have realized that sexual orientation is simply another part of diversity.

Besides RJR Nabisco, hundreds of additional gay and lesbian employee groups are forming at major American companies. They are all in varying degrees affecting the workplace policies and, in an increasing number of cases, the marketing planning of their respective companies in revolutionary ways.

The gay and lesbian employee group at AT&T, LEAGUE, co-authored with AT&T's marketing department an astonishingly shrewd and extremely effective 1994 direct-mail appeal for long-distance service aimed directly at gay and lesbian consumers.

The appeal was mailed in a lavender envelope and donned the image of a rainbow-colored phone cord on the outside, with an inside headline that read, "It's time for a change." The letter packaged with a brochure explaining AT&T's True USA Savings, True Rewards, and True Voice campaigns was signed by AT&T's Long Distance Service Manager and LEAGUE's two national co-chairs.

It even had a postscript, which read:

AT&T is pleased to be a part of Gay Games IV & Cultural Festival, taking place in New York City this June 18–25. Come to the Unity Center and receive a free gift.

Now, that is relationship marketing. It also represents one of the best possible examples of why the emerging gay and lesbian marketplace is really a gay and lesbian consumer revolution.

Although AT&T would not release sales figures for how well this particular campaign did, the company did retain Prime Access Inc., a firm run by Howard Buford, who was responsible for producing the ground-breaking advertising and direct-mail appeal that AT&T and LEAGUE collaborated on. According to Mr. Buford, who also advises American Express on gay and lesbian niche marketing and characterizes Prime Access Inc. as a full-service marketing and communications company providing management counsel in specialized markets:

You first want to get a feel for how comfortable a client is with different kinds of advertising in general. Does the client want ambiguous advertising vs. targeted advertising in this market? Sometimes they surprise you.

▼ ▼

From a business perspective, what tends to drive their corporate thinking [on gay and lesbian marketplace issues] has a lot to do with what each manager brings to the table. Each to a certain degree brings his or her own baggage to all the issues. A lot goes into the decision-making process—the manager's overall level of comfort, their background, their family—these things all impact on the overall strategy of the company.

There's also the issue of the way a company traditionally looks at markets or interprets risk—all of course which differs from company to company. Companies like AT&T want to be as appropriate as possible for as many people as possible.

This in essence should be the goal of any company that wants to reach the gay and lesbian consumer market: to be as appropriate as possible to as many people as possible.

In the emerging new world of global marketing, diversity politics, and hyper-competitiveness, the time will soon be upon us when few companies can afford to be seen as "inappropriate" with regard to the issues of sexual orientation in marketing.

There was a time in America's earlier years when racial exclusion was seen as appropriate. That changed. Excluding people based on their skin color is no longer appropriate. Likewise there was a time when it was perceived appropriate at nearly every level of society to repress people based on their sexual identity. That has changed as well. Repressing people based on their sexual orientation is no longer appropriate.

An important and increasingly influential national group called GLAAD, the Gay and Lesbian Alliance Against Defamation, whose expressed purpose is specifically to stop defamation of gay and lesbian Americans in the media, is gaining broad-scale public attention and the complete backing of mainstream business.

The GLAAD media awards are regularly hosted and attended by celebrity talent from across the performing and media arts spectrum (recently Phil Donahue and Marlo Thomas). Some of GLAAD'S accomplishments include a successful public relations campaign mounted against Cobb County, Georgia, for an anti–gay and lesbian ordinance. GLAAD's efforts in conjunction with public statements made by Olympic Gold Medalist Greg Louganis resulted in the moving of scheduled 1996 Olympic Events out of Cobb County. GLAAD was influential in helping the *New York Times* end its policy of banning the use of the word *gay* in its reporting.

GLAAD also convinced the CBS News affiliate in San Francisco to stop using the abusive and erroneous language such as "special rights" when reporting on controversial gay and lesbian discrimination ballot issues like Colorado's Amendment 2.

According to a recent flyer mailed to over 10,000 of GLAAD's supporters:

> Our monitoring, response, education, and visibility programs have changed the way society sees and represents gay, lesbian, and bisexual lives. . . .
>
> The *New York Times* wouldn't even let its reporters use the word "gay" ten years ago. Today, thanks to GLAAD the paper is an authority on the subject. So are its thousands of readers. . . .
>
> Hollywood's *Basic Instinct* kept filmmakers believing that gays and lesbians had to either be invisible or in jail. GLAAD helped them find us in *Philadelphia,* among other places.

In addition to preventing defamation of gays and lesbians in the media, GLAAD has also been successful in bringing together different groups within the gay and lesbian community to address a variety of issues related to the visibility of people of color.

Much of the advertising aimed at gay and lesbian Americans is often less than representative of the diversity of the entire gay and lesbian community—as is much of advertising overall. However, because gay and lesbian identity cuts across all social boundaries including race, religion, class, gender, and ethnicity, it becomes all the more important to deal with the imagery of gay and lesbian advertising much more sensitively and in a fashion that takes into consideration all the nuances, subtlety, and sophistication of gay and lesbian culture.

When these precautions are not taken, well-intentioned advertising aimed at gay and lesbian consumers can often come off being perceived as veiled racism, exclusionary, or smacking of various realms of social superiority.

Donald Suggs, director of communications for GLAAD, identifies some important issues in the use of race and gender in advertising and how marketing imagery often seeks, however ignorantly or purposefully, to pigeonhole gay and lesbian identity from a very "white" point of view—a view that some blacks see as homophobic and racist from an entirely different perspective.

▼ ▼

As Suggs notes:

I don't think most black gay people see the issue of homophobia in a vacuum. For us, it's part of a larger view of how [American culture] marginalizes a lot of people. Even straight white men get old, and eventually there's a way in which older people are marginalized in this culture. If you are really committed to struggling against homophobia, then you have to be committed to struggling against all the ways in which [our culture] marginalizes people. . . .

I think that black gay people have a better understanding of what that dynamic is. It's not just about being able to take your lover to the company picnic, [black people] see this whole array of ways in which this world has to be changed and transformed.

Most black gay people live within the black community, our perception of who we are is not predicated on being "out"; most black gay bars are located in the black community. Black people know those bars are there. Black people don't burn them down. I'm not saying the black community is less homophobic, I'm just saying we're homophobic in a different way. We don't define ourselves in a way that forces us to readjust or redefine what it means to be black or what your relationship to the community is. It does not take this form of you have to leave. I think in a lot of the white middle-class community you do have to leave [if you're gay or lesbian]. You have to move to New York, to San Francisco, or to a different neighborhood—I think that's homophobic, it's just expressing itself differently.

Also, homosexuality is seen in a different light [by black people]. For instance, if I meet some black men and ask if they are gay, they might say no. But if I say, are you "in the life," [it] incorporates this whole range of behaviors, ideas and self-perceptions that everyone encompasses. It is saying that you have an understanding.

Donald Suggs's remarks strike a chord that echo Linda Workman's about the emerging spectrum of diversity. Through the work of GLAAD, this diversity is having a cathartic effect within gay and lesbian culture as well as within the mainstream places where America's workers work, play, and reflect upon the imagery of media.

It is now a given that no company in America today would think of not making sure that their corporate policies are in line with the values of the majority of American citizens when it comes to issues of race, sex, and religion. The "emerging spectrum" simply now applies to sexual orientation as part of the evolutionary process of culture, work, family, and economics.

Americans are generally conservative people. But they are also humane and fair. As the gay and lesbian consumer revolution makes itself known more and more through media, politics, the workplace, and the marketplace, more Americans will come to see the ongoing fight for equal rights for gay and lesbian Americans as being simply basic to the "American experience" and our continually unfolding sense of heritage. And as noted earlier, the Yankelovich data shows that there is a consistent American trend signaling less animosity about gay and lesbian sexuality.

Old Stereotypes, New Information

Believe it or not, most gay and lesbian people are still relatively invisible in American society. While it is true that some gays and lesbians have sought to express certain modes of speech and dress, physical behaviors, and social attitudes that many might perceive as sterotypically gay or lesbian, such as the thin, lightweight male with feminine gestures (the sissy fag) or the heavyset female with masculine gestures (the butch dyke), these representations are representative of two different points on the continuum of heterosexual and homosexual behavior. By far, a larger proportion of Americans present themselves in their manner, dress, and speech in a way that is more representative of the social norm most people misconstrue as "heterosexual-looking."

When this truth is accepted, even gays and lesbians have to admit that they are not always aware of other gay and lesbian people around them. The point is that there are far more gay and lesbian people in the world than meets the eye. Which helps to explain why gay and lesbian visibility is such an integral part of the equal rights movement for gay and lesbian Americans. It also explains why groups like GLAAD and employee organizations at companies like RJR, Nabisco, and Apple have come into being.

Communicating with Gay and Lesbian Consumers:
The Right Products, the Right Approach

As outlined in the Yankelovich research in chapter 4, there are five general areas of significant difference that distinguish self-identifying gay and lesbian consumers from heterosexual consumers: a focus on individuality; a need for association; a search for life's diversity; the above average need to alleviate stress; and a pronounced sense of skepticism and mistrust of the social environment.

Within each of these areas (and in combination with each other) there is the extraordinary opportunity to position products and services that communicate specific benefits in relation to the differences indicated between gay consumers and straight consumers:

Focus on individuality

All products, goods, and services that relate to the consumer's sense of identity including clothing, shoes, jewelry, cosmetics, toiletries, health care, sports and fitness, home furnishings, books, magazines, travel, psychotherapy, hobbies, crafts, home study courses, etc.

Need for association

Restaurants, theaters, clubs, group travel, health and fitness, educational and trade institutions, spiritual and religious groups, arts and craft groups, sports clubs, dance clubs, arts and entertainment events, concerts, and public fund-raising drives.

Searching out and experiencing life's diversity

Pay-per-view television, interactive television, computers, on-line bulletin boards and communications venues, sporting events, weekend travel get-a-ways, virtual reality, community events, books, magazines, new restaurants, clubs, and entertainment opportunities. Theater, opera, music, dance, and performance art.

Stress alleviation

Sundries and packaged goods, music, bottled beverages, gourmet food and cooking supplies, sporting events, clothing and accessories, home sporting equipment, jogging shoes, massage therapy, acupuncture, psychotherapy, yoga, health clubs, weightlifting equipment, aromatherapy, arts and crafts, aerobics, gymnastics, swimming, hiking, and camping gear and clothing.

Skepticism and mistrust

Products that promote understanding and alleviate fear, home security systems, pets and pet care supplies, self-defense courses, financial services, and investment opportunities.

These are just a few of the products that stand to sell well to gay and lesbian consumers if marketed in a fashion that communicates individuality. In general, however, there are certain issues to bear in mind when developing campaigns for products and services aimed at this population.

General Strategy

Focusing soley on how great your company is in relationship to gay and lesbian employment issues is never in a company's best interest. It distracts from the product at hand and can lead to the suspicion that "thy company doth promote too much."

It is expected that your company is decent if you are already advertising to gay and lesbian consumers. When it comes to tooting a company's own horn in these areas, the understated "addendum approach" is best.

For instance, consider reserving your postscript in direct-marketing letters to remind gay or lesbian consumers that your company has domestic partnership benefits or supports a particular organization. However, playing up the issue too much makes it sound like you've done a favor for the consumer. Perhaps you have, but consumers want to give you their money for your good products and services and your "good name," not congratulations for your good moral deeds in the marketplace.

Focus first and foremost on your product or service and its benefits to the gay and lesbian consumer sense of perception. Give concrete examples of what you mean by quality. Cite how your product makes life easier, more enjoyable, fashionable, beautiful, comforting, etc. Explain the details that separate your product or service from your competition.

Don't be afraid to use humor. Some industries, such as fashion, food and beverage, and even home furnishings are able to pull off the use of aesthetic extremes such as unorthodox camera angles, wild lighting, good female impersonation, etc. Conservative companies, of course, should focus more seriously on product appeal, historical stature, and dependability.

But it must be remembered that gay and lesbian consumers are fast studies, quick to see through hollow appeals and misguided marketing. If a company has done its homework, has consulted

▼ ▼

with competent marketing counsel, and has encouraged the input of gay and lesbian employees or even customers, it will all shine through in the advertising and the sales.

Advertising and Direct Marketing Copy

As with most advertising copy, keeping it as short as possible is the general order of the times. With gay and lesbian consumers, even shorter is better.

As a rule, gay and lesbian consumers are discerning individuals. They get the point fast. So don't spend endless time getting to the point—unless the product or service genuinely demands a longer storyline. If you must incorporate a lot of copy into a print display advertisement or a direct-mail campaign, use boldface titles followed by short bullet points to break up the copy.

Advertising Imagery

Keep the use of canned gay and lesbian imagery to a minimum. Much of the commonly seen advertising aimed at gay and lesbian consumers today such as pink triangles, rainbow flags, and the use of lavender color have been a trend for the past eight years, but they are largely the domain of gay-and-lesbian-owned companies. This imagery means different things to different people.

The use of upside-down pink triangles (which the Nazis used in concentration camps to identify homosexuals) is risky. I would particularly advise against the use of pink triangles by any major corporation unless that corporation's history with gay and lesbian consumer is stellar clean. Marketers that dispute the sensitive nature of the use of pink triangles to attract gay and lesbian consumers might want to read Frank Rector's *The Nazi Extermination of Homosexuals* (Stein and Day, 1981) before sending a campaign to press with such symbolism. Few companies are in a strong enough moral or political position to sprinkle them around like computer-licensed clip art in their advertising and promotional campaigns. The risk of sending the wrong message is simply too great. And many older gay and lesbian Americans, particularly veterans, may be offended by their use on behalf of big business.

▼ ▼

Sending the Correct Message

Products and services advertised to gay and lesbian consumers must ultimately say two things:

- Our product is right for you.
- Our company is right for you.

Marketers do not have to reinvent the wheel or completely erase their creative drawing boards before attempting to map out a strategy for targeting gay and lesbian consumers. All of theorist Henry Murray's social motives still apply when advertising to gay and lesbian consumers—perhaps some even more so since this population cohort is particularly looking to "affiliate, achieve and understand."[8] The key is to communicate a matter-of-fact sense of understanding about gay and lesbian character in relationship to marketing services.

Remember Sensitivity

Marketers must not forget that in the back of every gay and lesbian consumer's mind is the accurate perception that, historically, mainstream society has not been tolerant of their individuality. There is also the potential that a sea of mixed feelings exists in the consumer's mind about sexual expression, social tolerance for sexual expression, its relation to AIDS and the public's perception of AIDS in relation to homosexuality. When a gay or lesbian consumer is confronted with marketing, imagery, and advertising messaging from your business, any background perceptions of the slightest hint of intolerance must be removed in relation to the company name or product branding.

These are politically charged times for gay and lesbian Americans. And each individual gay or lesbian person's experience, degree of outness, financial independence, etc., all impact on the perception of the brand and the willingness to respond to its positioning. These issues have changed and metamorphosed in the minds of gay and lesbian consumers over the past two decades, but especially so during the past ten years.

Prior to Randy Shilts's *And the Band Play On*, the best-selling gay-themed book was *The Joy of Gay Sex* and Jonathon Katz's *Gay*

▼ ▼

American History, which sold, according to its publisher, around 80,000–90,000 copies. Crown book editor Michael Denenny says that those figures "used to be my benchmark, if you had a best-seller in the gay and lesbian market you would get up around that."

What is particularly telling for marketers is what has occurred during the time between the days of *The Joy of Gay Sex* and *And the Band Played On.* About sixteen years.

Within that time period, hundreds of thousands of gay and lesbian Americans came out of the closet and celebrated in the gay and lesbian liberation movement in Modern America. In many ways, *The Joy of Gay Sex* symbolically represented, in marketing numbers, the celebration of that social unfolding.

But the numbers are equally telling in the way the story has ended for so many. And this is a fact that has remained resident in the gay/lesbian consumer mind.

In that short sixteen years is the representation of the enormity of the AIDS crisis and the horror of its devastation, book-ended by sales figures that speak for themselves and cast a broad-ranging commentary on gay and lesbian culture—particularly gay male urban culture. Two best-selling books, at the beginning and end of that sixteen years, one that confirmed the birth of gay liberation, the other chronicling what has become death in numbers greater than all who died in all of the American wars of this century.

The parallels between gay and lesbian visibility and the AIDS crisis pervades much of the issues of this community. This must be remembered by marketers.

Michael Denneny, who edited *And the Band Played On* for St. Martin's, as well as many other successful gay and lesbian titles, states, "I can remember in 1967 when three gay men could not congregate on a street corner. Stonewall was only twenty-five years ago, and I've been only publishing gay books for sixteen years, the difference in the sixteen years is enormous. I'm concerned about the consolidation of the gay audience, the gay imagination, the consolidation of the gay spiritual life, for want of a better term.

Marketers need to ask themselves important questions in relation to what the "consolidation of the gay audience" means to them.

To target gay and lesbian Americans as consumers is to target America's youth, America's war veterans, parents, brothers and sisters, people of color, Jews, Christians, Hispanics, those with disabilities, people living with HIV, AIDS, or breast cancer. To target gay and lesbian Americans is to conduct business with many different groups of people—the Mature Generation, Baby Boomers, and the Generation Xers. It's building a consumer relationship with people who are cynical about "consumer relations." It's about conducting business with many who are perpetually grieving for the loss of an entire generation of their friends and loved ones to AIDS—particularly Baby Boomers.

In 1994, the Chrysler Corporation posted $3.7 billion in total profits. Yet not a single dollar of the profit that was obtained was acquired through the targeted advertising of automobiles to gay and lesbian Americans.

Nothing against Chrysler. No American car manufacturer did. But gay and lesbian Americans know that as well. They also know that most packaged goods manufacturers, food companies, hair care products producers, and home furnishings companies did not target them as well. Which is why they'll pay particular attention to SAAB, Saturn, IKEA, and Procter & Gamble, which recently made their forays into the gay and lesbian marketplace. They will be remembered.

Gay and lesbian consumers notice every new product that is being marketed directly to them. But gay and lesbian Americans also have long memories. Those born during the war years have a history of feelings and perspectives about gay liberation that runs differently, sometimes counter to, those born in the Reagan years. They very much remember the homosexual witch-hunts of the 1950s, McCarthy, the Stonewall Riots, Anita Bryant, and the impact of the orange juice boycott.[9]

Younger gay and lesbian Amerians—particularly teenagers and some Generation Xers, don't know this history. It's not taught in the schools of America. So they are more responsive to niche advertising aimed at them with less of the cynicism associated with their older peers.

Although AIDS and civil rights struggles have touched the lives of Americans of all ages and sexual orientations across the country, no group has been more affected, battered, and burdened with the grief of AIDS than the gay and lesbian community. Advertisers and marketers must bear this in mind when developing nearly any marketing campaign designed to raise awareness of a given product or service to gay and lesbian consumers. By no means does this mean to say that every advertising message has to serve a socially and

▼ ▼

politically correct cause—but is does have to be "emotionally informed" from a sense of realism about modern gay and lesbian culture.

Which brings us to the development and portrayal of accurate images and characterizations of gay and lesbian consumers in marketing and advertising communications.

Verisimilitude

Consider an innocently placed advertisement for a restaurant in a local gay and lesbian news publication showing two muscle-studded white boys in tank tops spoon-feeding each other strawberries dripping in whipped cream. It may appeal to some, but if it does not run concurrently every other week showing women and people of color in the same scenario, it may be driving a certain clientele of business away from your establishment.

Just before turning in this manuscript, I saw an advertisement on the side of a truck in New York that showed a beautiful man dancing with a beautiful woman. The man was wearing a tuxedo and the woman was wearing a long flowing gown. They had smiles on their faces. It was truly a beautiful picture. Then I noticed the headline, which read, "Man At His Best."

The implication was subtle, but indicative of why gay and lesbian consumers are cynical about advertising, media imagery, and mainstream culture in general. The advertisement could have been made all the more shrewd and potentially less insulting if it simply had said, "*A* Man At His Best," meaning the singular man in the picture, a single example of "a man" at "his" personal best for him—not all men.

This is the kind of mistake that marketers cannot afford to make when targeting gay and lesbian consumers.

No doubt, equal opportunity advertising does not have to be the rule when it comes to marketing. Not all products and services are intended for everyone. And not all products and services can be successfully marketed to gay and lesbian consumers. But an advertisement in New York City is no place to make mistakes about gay and lesbian consumers. The key is, strike a happy medium between the representation of social and sexual diversity in marketing imagery and who the product or service is likely to impact the most.

▼ ▼

Details magazine is particularly adept at striking this sensitive balance in both its imagery and editorial copy. The editors have a solid understanding of who their market is: men—gay and straight—and some women, and they direct their energies toward casting a wide enough net not to offend anyone yet focus on enough specifics to attract a broad range of men and women.

This philosophy is even in their name. Mark Healy, an editor at *Details*, says, "Sensitivity is an issue. We wouldn't do something if it's going to offend a certain segment of the population—any segment of the population. At *Details*, there's a '*Details* guy' that everyone sort of has in the back of his mind. And I think that he can be pretty bisexual."

It's no secret that young gay men like *Details*. Yet it is not known as a gay man's magazine; nor is it known as a magazine for "good ol' boys." It is a magazine for all men.

Striking a balance between diversity and the demands of product positioning and budgeting is not easy. The highly successful *Out*, a mainstream general interest magazine focusing on culture, media, politics, and a host of other interests and issues relevant to nearly the entire social spectrum of gay and lesbian America, is faced each month with striking one of the most challenging balances in the entire gay and lesbian marketplace. It must constantly strive to be inclusive of the entire spectrum of diversity in culture—not only of gay and lesbian America, but of life itself—as gays and lesbians "perceive it."

Be Matter-of-Fact

Not every gay-targeted product needs a gay spin in its print advertising, but it does have to avoid any suggestion of appearing as if it is afraid to be what it is—an ad in a gay publication! Therefore, don't make the mistake of placing an ad in a gay publication that shows heterosexual coupling exclusively. At the same time, don't be afraid to be aggressive in your messaging and aggressive in your product positioning.

As Michael Kaminer of Michael Kaminer Publications—a firm with a solid track record in handling publicity for gay and straight clients alike along with the successful *Out* magazine—remarks, "I approach and handle gay publications the way I handle my other accounts. I'm as aggressive as possible. It all requires micromanage-

▼ ▼

ment but at the same time I cast as wide a net as possible. I never assume anybody is homophobic, I never assume anybody will hang up on me. *Out* is respected immensely; it does not have a code word for being gay; even its title is about as *out* as you can get."

And Mr. Kaminer's take regarding the use of coding to attract gay consumers: "I hate coding. If you're going to go after this market, don't insult, don't use euphemisms. Gay consumers have some of the strongest bullshit detectors around."

In the first issue of *Out* (launched in the summer of 1992), editors Michael Goff and Sarah Pettit characterized what they were setting out to do with the magazine, writing, "*Out* comes from many viewpoints within a spectrum—stylish and substantial, serious and frivolous, classic and new, highbrow and trashy, necessary and unexpected—all with gay and lesbian treated as matter-of-fact."

Matter-of-fact is the operative phrase. It is particularly important when targeting gay and lesbian consumers to present images of gay and lesbian people "as they really are." This is why businesses and marketers new to the gay and lesbian world of consumerism need to rely on a level of community involvement—to insure that the aesthetics and terminology being used in the marketing message is indicative of verisimilitude.

Two and a half years later, *Out* is still focused on being as candid and as matter-of-fact as possible in their communication and representation of gay and lesbian life, issues, and questions. According to Goff, "We've had two major marches in two years, we're entrenched in our ghettos and establishments, we're settling in for the long AIDS haul, and a new generation is finding it a bit easier to come of age. We are even taking on the difficult issue of defining ourselves as a community.

"But as individuals we're left in a quagmire of conflicting self-definition—balancing the gay and lesbian worlds that we gratefully, and often unquestioningly, fall into. And we've all faced the difficulties of growing up gay or lesbian. We don't have the benefit of parents and forebears to instill in us a sense of what it means to be gay in America—the mentoring that other minorities take for granted. So it's a bit harder."

For marketers, it is important to be able to communicate an understanding of, as Goff characterizes, "the quagmire of conflicting self-definition." But still, as all marketers know, mistakes happen.

▼ ▼

Comprehensive Marketing

Not all campaigns work. Some are great. Some are flops. It is important to be able to defend your marketing decisions and philosophies from a position of authority based on real research, informed intellectual contribution from gay and lesbian business, and community authorities. The goal is to stay ever mindful that marketing products and services to gay and lesbian Americans requires a sober understanding of and ability to project accurate imagery in the commercial marketplace.

Jeanne Cordova, publisher of the *Los Angeles Gay and Lesbian Community Yellow Pages,* which is chocked with every kind of advertising imaginable and fills a much needed and unique niche in Southern California, says, "What major companies need to do to is become more informed about lesbian sensibility, [they need to show] two women together or single women dressed the way a lesbian [might] dress."

Ms.Cordova, who had her own publication in the 1970s called *Lesbian Tide,* also agrees that there is a connection between being aligned with the gay and lesbian community and conducting business with gay and lesbian consumers. Commenting about women's issues in particular, she said, "Companies need to be willing to make contributions specifically to lesbian groups."

This is one of the most important issues that marketers do not address. There are more women in the world than there are men. Suffice to say, then, that there are most likely at least as many lesbians as gay men (this notion is buttressed by Yankelovich research).

If you're marketing exclusively to gay men, then you're missing half of the marketplace. If you're only making contributions to AIDS organizations, thinking that that makes your company supportive of the gay and lesbian community, you are only partially right. If you're not making any contributions to any gay or lesbian organizations, are you seeking appropriate marketing consultation regarding the gay and lesbian marketplace in the geographic area or industry you're targeting? Can you afford not to do this?

In the bigger picture of gay and lesbian politics and history, there is a profound dynamic between AIDS philanthropy in general and the gay and lesbian community. Jay Blotcher, an activist and writer from New York, characterizes the issue regarding AIDS in an interesting way, that there is a relation between marketing and the gay

▼ ▼

and lesbian fight for visibility, equal rights, and an end to the AIDS crisis. He says:

> *You have to go back to the connection between AIDS and this market. You'd be hard-pressed to say what AIDS did that was good for the community, but it did spark this amazing awareness—awareness that forced people out of the closet and forced a mainstream consciousness of gays and lesbians. It brought people out.*
>
> *If you look at old copies of* After Dark *in the mid-seventies, marketing to gay people was happening in a big way, and I would contend that AIDS is what dropped the big black curtain on it all in the early eighties. Because in the 1970s mainstream fashion and films, colognes, etcetera, were putting money into this community. It was already happening long before AIDS.*

Mr. Blotcher is absolutely right. All through the 1970s, *After Dark,* a national entertainment magazine with an overwhelmingly gay and lesbian readership (a kind of loose and somewhat politically incorrect version of *Out* for the bell-bottom years) enjoyed major attention from all kinds of high-profile advertisers.

The pages of *After Dark* enjoyed advertisers reflective of that era: Metro-Goldwyn-Mayer; RCA Records; Paramount Pictures, then a subsidiary of Gulf & Western; Columbia Pictures; Twentieth-Century Fox; Warner Brothers; Carnegie Hall; and the New York City Ballet.

Liquor was being advertised in the pages of *The Advocate;* the Hearst Corporation had begun printing paperbacks of interest to gay and lesbian consumers through their Avon Books division; Bantam was offering seven different books as well—one of which was *The Front Runner* by Patricia Warren. The rights to the film were purchased by Paul Newman. And book publishers were already printing at least ten times as many gay/lesbian-themed books than the period prior to the Stonewall Riots.

In New York City new luxury high-rise residences were openly marketing their exclusive real estate to gay and lesbian consumers. As early as 1975, the *Wall Street Journal* reported on these developments in an article entitled "Campaigns to Sell to Homosexual Market Are Being Launched by More Big Firms":[10]

> This might have been hard to imagine only a few years ago. But today, American business is starting once-unthinkable projects—campaigns to reach the homosexual market. The trend is spotty, but dozens of major companies are taking steps.

▼ ▼

As an interesting commentary on how times have changed, the same article quoted a Bloomingdale's spokesperson on what was then a fashionable line of new products, licensed by the Continental Baths of New York City:

> Other industries are getting involved, too. Bloomingdale's, a leading New York department store, last summer offered a line of towels carrying the imprint of Continental Baths, a well-known homosexual sauna in the city. The store says they sold so well that Bloomingdale's decided to stock a whole special section with Continental Bath T-shirts, sweat shirts and other items. It also brought out a line of beach towels imprinted with "Cherry Grove" or "Fire Island Pines.". . .
>
> "This is one of the campiest things we have ever done," says a spokeswoman. "This is the time for products with a camp appeal. I don't think our executives were particularly worried about it. I doubt we'll attract any more gay customers than we already have."

Times are clearly different. And marketers need to stay ever mindful that they are dealing with sensitive issues in a sensitive era when they go about promoting products and services to gay consumers. Yet they do not need to handle gay and lesbian consumers with kid gloves. There is no need to walk on eggshells with marketing messaging. It is important to be matter-of-fact with the message, not conflicted. Coded subtly, as in shrewdly constructed inclusiveness, is one thing; seeking to create overly closeted imagery or double messaging that a company can then "deny as being gay or lesbian" is quite another. Gay and lesbian consumers often recognize the difference.

Changing Times, Again

American gay and lesbian cultural struggle has, on differing levels, always been connected to the politics of minority economics. Marketers should accept that as a modern influential phenomenon, gay and lesbian consumerism continues to be intimately aligned with gay and lesbian activism—this has especially been the case during the past five years. Mr. Blotcher addresses this marketing trend as well."[1]

> *[It] started up again in the late 80s. There are so many things that [happened], gay people were turning into a political force and a culture force after*

▼ ▼

Stonewall. It was about the clubs and the clothes. About 1989, 1990, sud-denly it was our world again, Andy Rooney stuff, the rappers doing anti-gay stuff, marketing started again. . . . It was all beginning to resurge with AIDS activism, Queer Nation, and the films that were coming out. . . . But then again, with the awareness, gays and lesbians weren't happy with Basic Instinct *and they were unhappy about* Silence of the Lambs. . . .

And then the boycotts. It's disputable what impact the boycotts have had specifically, but the awareness was coming out. And as always, change does not start just with gays, it starts with the arts, so we were very shrewd in ACT-UP, but also with Queer Nation. We knew that the arts eventually affects everything else. More changes of heart come with a good film than a law being passed. Philadelphia *did more for activism and AIDS than all the demon-strations up until then. . . .*

[Then] people broke into Burroughs Wellcome, and bolted themselves into a room, handcuffed themselves saying they were going to have a standoff and stay in there until 'you lower the price of AZT,' and within an hour they were dragged out by the police. . . . That was the beginning.

Then . . . came the demo at the Stock Exchange. All that stuff, not letting up the pressure, finally sparked the media, including the New York Times *editorial on greediness and profit mongering [of Burroughs Wellcome], and when the* New York Times *is creating nicks in your shining reputation, that's when things change. That's when Burroughs Wellcome cried uncle and lowered the price [of AZT]. News is one thing, gay stuff creeping into main-stream sitcoms is the legacy of activism. We're making gay issues a big deal now, so one day they won't have to be.*

▼ ▼

CHAPTER 6

RAINBOW TARGET MARKETING

Insights and Opportunities for Business

A company that puts back into the community is going to win no matter what.

FRANCIS STEVENS, EDITOR, *DENEUVE*

A new window of opportunity is now presenting itself to American businesses that are willing to target gay and lesbian consumers. By having a general undertanding of the developing economic trends and cultural innovations that are occurring within the gay and lesbian marketplace, companies can begin to grasp how their products and services might best be positioned for long-term appeal and solid brand-loyalty development.

Key Cities and Specific Neighborhoods

To target gay and lesbian consumers is to target America's cities—both large and small. The greatest cross section of self-identifying gay and lesbian Americans live in the cities. And like heterosexual Americans, they spend, on average, the greatest portion of their total income on rental housing or homeowner mortgages.

National real estate brokerage firms have not yet made a serious effort to market to gays and lesbians as a target group through gay and lesbian media. Yet real estate and rental property plays an

▼ ▼

important role in the maintenance and growth of gay and lesbian neighborhoods across America. In addition, the majority of America's gay and lesbian newspapers are located in the highest-valued property areas of the country, yet generally charge the least expensive rates per column inch of advertising space for those areas.

Independent real estate agents report that the presence of gays and lesbians in certain areas of the country actually increases property values. They further report that gays and lesbians often help rejuvenate small neighborhood economies—many of which later become important areas of business commerce and long-term urban and cultural renewal.

The explosion of neighborhood revitalization in relation to gay and lesbian consumerism in cities across the United States has been documented in many major newspapers across the country. Strong gay and lesbian neighborhoods also attract business and conventions to cities that might not otherwise enjoy such a large influx of revenue.

Last year, the *New York Times* reported on this phenomenon in "Gay Presence Leads Revival of Declining Neighborhoods":

> Predominantly gay neighborhoods have arisen in a dozen major cities over the last two decades, at once bolstering those cities' sagging tax bases, pumping thousands of dollars into the economy, and sometimes making tired neighborhoods safer and more attractive to heterosexuals.
>
> Sociologists and demographers alike say the concentration of homosexuals in core neighborhoods has grown in the last two decades out of gay political advocacy and the AIDS crisis, as well as from generally more tolerant attitudes toward homosexuals. That visibility has translated into demarcated gay neighborhoods whose residents demand recognition. . . .
>
> [In] Oklahoma City, where the International Gay Bowling League and the International Gay Rodeo Association stage annual events . . . Steve Collier, the executive director of the Oklahoma City Convention and Visitors Bureau, [says] the two events accounted for hotel bookings of several thousand rooms. Mark S. Schwartz, a member of the Oklahoma City Council whose ward has the most visible gay population in the city, said: "They bring in a lot of people, and that helps the local economy. Their deposits look the same, their taxes look the same."[1]

▼ ▼

This rise in stature in gay/lesbian neighborhoods across America has had an immeasurable effect on the growth and stability of pivotal inner-city neighborhoods. There is a down side, however. With the rise of visibility in these areas—many of which include homes from the turn of the century valued in the millions of dollars—there has been the added perpetuation of the stereotype that gays and lesbians are more affluent than they really are.

This local visibility, of gay and lesbian Americans living in affluent or "fashionable" neighborhoods, combines with the distorted rhetoric of right-wing radicals and misrepresented gay newspaper market research statistics to leave the impression that gay and lesbian Americans have more money than they actually do. While it is true that tens of thousands of gays and lesbians are homeowners in the United States, so are heterosexuals—hundreds of thousands— in the cities.

That challenge aside, as a group, gays and lesbians tend to move to larger urban areas where property values eventually become higher. This trend was especially noticeable, from 1972–1995, in the following areas:

- Montrose and Heights in Houston
- Oaklawn in Dallas
- Cheesman Park area in Denver
- Seattle's Capitol Hill
- Liberty Hill in Cincinatti
- The Grand Street area in St. Louis
- Greenwich Village, Chelsea, SoHo, Brooklyn Heights, and Park Slope in New York City
- Hollywood, West Hollywood, Silverlake, and Venice Beach in Los Angeles
- Andersonville and Lakeview in Chicago
- Lockerbie Square and the Near North Side of Indianapolis
- Ft. Lauderdale and South Beach in Miami
- Dupont Circle in Washington, D.C.
- Northern Liberties area and Graduate Hospital/South of South Street in Philadelphia
- Numerous neighborhoods in San Francisco

▼ ▼

Of the entire self-identified gay and lesbian population in the United States, more are likely to own homes in larger urban areas because such areas are simply more known for being—or are within driving distance of—widely recognized gay and lesbian centers of culture.

The neighborhoods listed above will continue to be important gay and lesbian population growth regions into the next century. The following cities can also be expected to experience a fast and profound level of gay and lesbian population growth throughout the next century: Baltimore, Maryland; Jacksonville, Tampa, and St. Petersburg in Florida; Atlanta and Savannah, Georgia; Corpus Christi, Austin, El Paso, Ft. Worth, and San Antonio in Texas; Sacramento, San Diego, San Jose, Monterey, Long Beach, and Palm Springs in California; New Orleans; Minneapolis/St.Paul; Columbus, Ohio; Portland, Oregon; Nashville and Memphis, Tennessee; Albuquerque; Madison and Milwaukee in Wisconsin; Philadelphia, Pittsburgh, and New Hope, Pennsylvania; Boston and Provincetown, Massachusetts; Little Rock, Arkansas; Providence, Rhode Island; Bloomington, Indiana; Detroit, Michigan; Greenwich, Connecticut; various areas on Long Island, New York, and areas most heavily populated in New Jersey from Hoboken to the shore; Charlotte, North Carolina; Honolulu; Oklahoma City; and Kansas City, Missouri.

Each of these areas is experiencing new surges of gay and lesbian cultural visibility, and most offer a lower cost of living as well, making them attractive places for gay and lesbian Americans to reside in as an alternative to the larger gay and lesbian "mecca cities."

Cashing In with Food and Drink

Gay and lesbian Americans spend the second largest portion of their total income on food and beverages—whether purchased in restaurants and clubs or as groceries from local area supermarkets.

Alcoholic beverages, restaurants, and clubs, combined with other small retail and service-oriented businesses, make up the largest proportion of display advertising in gay and lesbian publications across the country.

While there is no reason to believe that gays and lesbians would not clip savings coupons for groceries from local gay and lesbian

▼ ▼

newspapers, relatively few grocery chains take advantage of the opportunities gay and lesbian newspapers offer for the advertisement of groceries. No major food chain to date has launched a broad-scale gay and lesbian advertising campaign. This marks one of the most untapped market niches in the entire food and beverage industry—especially in light of Yankelovich data showing gay/lesbian interest in gourmet cooking, home entertaining, and the home in general as a place of security and community socializing.

Local area restaurants, however, especially those owned and operated in predominantly gay- and lesbian-populated neighborhoods, have enjoyed monumental success advertising their businesses in local gay and lesbian newspapers.

The average start-up cost for a mid-size restaurant in the United States is around $200,000. Weekly revenue in a busy restaurant can even out around thirty to forty thousand in well-populated locations. With the average quarter-page advertisement in most gay and lesbian news weeklies running less than two hundred and fifty dollars, newly opened restaurants would be smart to make advertising to the gay and lesbian market a major priority.

A new restaurant's success or failure often hinges on an understanding of and marketing to gay and lesbian consumers. This is not necessarily because gay and lesbian consumers are more likely to eat out, but because for a given geographic area they may represent the largest cross section of the entire population—meaning African-Americans and other minorities, Generation Xers, Baby Boomers, and Matures, families, businesspeople, etc.

In the beverage industry, the trend toward segmentation of advertising spending is seen in the promotion of bottled water through sponsorship of gay and lesbian events and advertising in gay and lesbian publications. In 1987, Naya Water from Nora Beverage Company was the first bottled water to be openly targeted to gays and lesbians. A regional campaign was promoted through the gay and lesbian press, and since that time Nora Beverages has promoted Naya at gay and lesbian pride celebrations each year.

According to Stu Levenson, vice president of Nora Beverages, "We try and keep away from politics or direct social commentary on groups in general, but support basic human rights.

Indeed they do. Naya Water maintained and even heightened its visibility within the gay and lesbian community when it launched a

▼ ▼

shrewd marketing effort at a critically important time for gays and lesbians: Naya provided complimentary water at the gay and lesbian March on Washington in April 1993.

Evidently the other water bottlers are beginning to wise up. By 1994 Nora Beverages began to see the emergence of its competitors to the gay and lesbian market across the United States—including Evian, Perrier, and Calistoga. According to Levenson, the drivers on sales routes across the country still report increasing sales of Naya Water in known gay and lesbian neighborhoods. It is clear that gays and lesbians know who supported them first and are continuing to purchase Naya Bottled Water out of loyalty.

Since food and beverage industries comprise the second largest area of gay and lesbian spending in the United States, other food and beverage producers, restaurants, grocery stores, and convenience marts should consider aiming their products at gays and lesbians—particularly through gay and lesbian regional newspapers, while brand-loyalty establishment time is still available. Quarterly and annually printed regional gay and lesbian advertiser guides, Yellow Pages (both gay and those printed by the phone companies), and neighborhood directories also provide excellent ways to reach gay and lesbian consumers across the country.

According to Rob Davis, president and publisher of the highly successful *Metrosource,* a comprehensive magazinelike community resource of businesses in the New York City metropolitan area, "The people that advertise in *Metrosource* tell us they get results. [Our] ideal advertiser is service oriented.

"I know you've heard this before, but there is a segment of the population that really wants to support the people that advertise in gay and lesbian publications. There are a lot of gay and lesbian consumers out there who feel that if a company is genuinely being supportive, that their products and services should be bought first. Obviously it's in my interest to believe that, but I think that because of people's pride in the community they want to support products that are being aimed at them."

Absolut Vodka learned that lesson long ago as one of the first leading alcoholic beverage products to be marketed to gay and lesbian consumers. Michel Roux, president and CEO of Carillon Importers, Ltd., was one of the pioneers in advertising who helped bring heightened brand visibility and a dependable source of revenue to gay and lesbian publications in the United States. It was through Michel Roux's import company that Absolut, Gran Marnier, and Bombay Gin first made their appearances in *The Advocate* in the late 1970s.

Although Absolut is still the number-one vodka choice for gays and lesbians (and non-gay consumers as well), Carillon lost its distribution rights to Absolut when Vin & Spirit, the Swedish state-owned producer, abruptly moved the Absolut brand to Seagram. Since that time Roux moved to acquire the distribution rights to Stolichnaya vodka, which was the leading brand prior to Roux's miracle work with Absolut.

Roux, in association with advertising agency Margeotes, Fertitta, Donaher and Weiss, has produced a compelling campaign for Stolichnaya, which is also making use of the gay and lesbian consumer marketplace to compete against Absolut.

Roux's marketing philosophy regarding the gay and lesbian marketplace has still not changed. He commented in *Next News,* a gay marketing news magazine, last year, "In time, people will realize we are there and that we are supporting the gay community. It takes a further commitment. A marketer should also be supporting the gay community in areas such as civil rights, AIDS research, and political equality." Under Roux's stewardship, the Stoli brand has associated itself with DIFFA (Design Industry Foundation for AIDS), God's Love We Deliver (a nonprofit service providing meals to people with AIDS), and the North American Gay Volleyball Association Championship Tournament.

Other leading alcoholic beverages include Miller, Budweiser, Rolling Rock, Amstel Light, Remy Martin, Hennessy Cognac, Dewars White Label Scotch, Godiva Liqueur, and Campari—all of which have advertised in the major national gay and lesbian publications. There are many others.

It should be noted that gays and lesbians are shown in some survey data to participate in a higher consumption of tobacco-related products, although tobacco companies have traditionally shied away from buying advertising in gay and lesbian publications. In 1994, Parliament and Benson & Hedges advertising began to appear in *Out* magazine. Marlboro and Winston outdoor advertising is also relatively conspicuous in gay and lesbian neighborhoods around the country.

▼ ▼

Health & Fitness Opportunities

Entire books have been written on gay and lesbian health care, AIDS, and the relationships between the politics of big business marketing and the bureaucracy of government involvement (or lack of involvement).

The state of health care in the gay and lesbian community exists at a distinct disadvantage in comparison to the health care enjoyed by heterosexuals—mainly to the extent that most gays and lesbians cannot share employment-related health care benefits with their lovers or companions in the same way that heterosexuals can with their legally recognized spouses. This presents problems in many gay families.

As indicated previously in this book, in some companies this is changing. Domestic partnership benefits in the workplace allow unmarried partners to sign up for benefits through group health insurance programs in the same way that heterosexual married partners do. According to Richard Mayora, an account executive at HBO and a coordinator with the Time Warner gay and lesbian employee group, domestic partnership benefits became available at HBO in July of 1993. "It was the chairman's decision. He thought it was the equitable thing to do."

At that time, Time Warner owned forty-four different companies including Time Inc., *Time* magazine, Home Box Office, Warner Music Group, Warner Pictures, Time-Warner Cable, Atlantic Records, Elektra and Sire records—not all of which have domestic partnership benefits, for a variety of organizational and financial reasons too lengthy to discuss here.

Mayora characterizes the environment in this way: "You're talking about forty-four different companies at Time Warner—in many cases, very different from each other, with differing corporate climates. At HBO specifically, management has been topnotch in every way in terms of policies, [particularly] AIDS, and very understanding when it comes to benefits."

Considering the monumental amount of work, frustration, and rage that activists, health care professionals, caregivers, and families and friends have felt, AIDS as a marketplace issue cannot possibly be discussed or even remotely characterized in a preliminary fashion within the context of this book without insulting the experiences, challenges, hardships, and grief being experienced by the gay and lesbian community in general.

▼ ▼

The fact still remains: AIDS has hit the gay and lesbian community hard, and it is now enveloping the country's African-American and Hispanic-American communities. The crisis is taking a toll at a number of socioeconomic levels and raises enormous questions about the state of health care and its relationship to democracy and leadership in the United States overall. (A number of books are listed in the bibliography that have begun to address these issues as they relate to marketplace dynamics.)

Because health care within the gay and lesbian community cannot be looked at without including all the marketplace issues related to AIDS, breast cancer, heart disease, etc., it would be hard to place a dollar value or emphasis on key areas of growth. Clearly there are health-related industries that are targeting gay and lesbian consumers—most visibly, major insurance and health care providers, private practice physicians and specialized medical professionals, viatical service insurance brokers (specialists who broker life insurance policies), pharmaceuticals, health and fitness foods, vitamins, and private psychotherapy. But the fact that many of these industries' financial relationship is more associated with AIDS than gay and lesbian target marketing cannot be denied. (More is discussed regarding this issue at the end of the chapter.)

The 1970s and 1980s saw a pronounced increase in the number of psychotherapists offering their services exclusively to gay and lesbian consumers. In light of the Yankelovich analysis of the psychology of disenfranchisement in chapter 4, it would not seem farfetched to say that gays and lesbians are spending disproportionate dollars on maintaining their mental and physical health.

In addition, every major gay and lesbian community in the United States can claim several gyms or exercise facilities that cater predominantly to gay and lesbian health and sports enthusiasts. The Los Angeles metropolitan area alone has at least ten different gyms and sports facilities with an almost exclusive gay or lesbian clientele. Some are gay-owned, promoted, and operated. The same can be said for New York, Chicago, San Francisco, and Miami.

This continuing phenomenon of a focus on health in gay communities presents open opportunities for manufacturers of sportswear and sports equipment, as well as health-related food and beverage products.

▼ ▼

Entertainment

Because gay and lesbian Americans have a strong need to connect within their community, entertainment—not surprisingly—is fueling marketplace activity in areas that are literally too many to mention. The most obvious and consistent phenomenon of entertainment, dating back to the nineteenth century, is the gay bar.

In smaller communities where there are no gay and lesbian community centers, the gay bar is still an especially important social institution for gays and lesbians. It is a principal area of interest for cigarette, beer, and liquor distributors as well as the restaurants, gift shops, hardware stores, pet supply stores, and pharmacies that cater to gay and lesbian consumers in those neighborhoods where such bars are located.

Although less of a social focus in large cities than in previous years, gay and lesbian nightclubs, restaurants, dance halls, and bars still constitute a major focus of economic activity in mid-size and smaller cities across the United States.

Clothing

The 1990s finally saw the emergence of preliminary fashion advertising aimed directly at gay and lesbian consumers through print media purchased in gay and lesbian publications. Part of this trend is related to a relaxation of some of the leading fashion designers' attitudes toward gay and lesbian newspaper and magazine publishing's long history of being well supported by sexually oriented advertising. As such advertising has begun to disappear from the pages of national gay and lesbian publications, the fashion advertising appears to have likewise increased.

By far, *Out*, which has never accepted sexually oriented advertising, has set the modern tone and put the wheels in motion to attract and keep new advertisers, particularly fashion advertisers. Harry Taylor, formerly advertising director and now publisher of *Out*, has had a historical influence in this particular area. According to Mr. Taylor, one reason *Out* has been successful, particularly in new advertising areas, is that a large portion of the staff came from mainstream publications where the professional environment, aesthetic standards, and marketplace competition was much tougher than the environments traditionally found at many gay and lesbian publishing firms.

▼ ▼

Harry Taylor says that in earlier years "the gay and lesbian magazine industry suffered in the eyes of advertisers as looking 'the way that gay media looked'—less than professional, production quality not up to par, inundated with sexually oriented advertising, editorial quality below that of mainstream media." Those publications were "basically compiled by well-intended people who were doing the best service they possibly could based on the funds they were being paid."

According to Taylor, *Out* changed all that. Indeed, some manufacturers and fashion designers of men's and women's clothing are more openly courting the gay and lesbian consumer market— either through the pages of *Out* and other gay and lesbian publications, or through mainstream fashion and lifestyle publications, outdoor advertising, and direct-mail efforts.

One particular company, once famous for pushing cotton durables in a faux jungle atmosphere, produced a series of ads showing same-sex couples holding each other in forlorn romantic poses. The campaign was not bad, and it garnered a lot of attention and support from gay and lesbian consumers. But then all of a sudden it disappeared.

Since then that same company has caustically declined to confirm or deny that any of its marketing approaches ever had anything to do with gays or lesbians specifically.

I believe this kind of push-pull, mixed-message sending is partially responsible for the gay and lesbian consumers' cynicism and mistrust of business in general. Perhaps patterns for certain companies will alter themselves with the changing seasons.

Gay and Lesbian Travel Is Booming

Gays and lesbians travel a lot. Both domestically and overseas.

This fact presents enormous opportunities for marketers—especially in areas known for gay and lesbian vacation travel within the United States, such as Los Angeles, San Francisco, New York, Provincetown, Massachusetts, Key West and Miami, New Orleans, Louisiana, Seattle, Hawaii, the U.S. Virgin Islands, Atlanta, and Washington D.C.

There are hundreds of gay/lesbian-owned travel agencies operating in the United States, with some 330 registered specifically with the IGTA (International Gay Travel Association). In a recent

▼ ▼

survey of all travel agent members in which 104 responded (77 owners or independent contractors, 27 employees), $324,389,000 in business per year was reported, or an average of $3,119,125 per responding business. Since the survey (conducted in 1994), the IGTA's membership has doubled.

Clearly, the travel industry is one of the leading and more progressive industries affecting gay and lesbian economies, policies, and business marketing decisions in important companies in the United States. More and more airlines, car rental agencies, and tour groups are now aligning themselves favorably with gay and lesbian travelers.

Things are looking good and changing rapidly according to John Dellassandro, president of Out & Travel—a specialist in the domestic and international gay and lesbian travel market and adviser to American Airlines and Northwest Airlines:

I would have to make this point, there are two airlines that come to mind very quickly as very 'pro.' I have to say first and foremost that Virgin Atlantic is a major player within this market, even though many don't see them as a major domestic player . . . And of course, are you sitting down? American Airlines.

American Airlines provides a very interesting scenario. I hate even mentioning it, but American Airlines in many ways took a very serious look at the gay and lesbian marketplace because of negative incidents that happened.

Three negative instances took place during the past few years. One involved the alleged firing of an employee based on sexual orientation. The second surrounded the nationally reported debacle over the forced removal of an American Airlines passenger with AIDS. The third, and perhaps most pivotal, was the changing of linens on an aircraft that had completed its scheduled flight to Washington, D.C., during the 1993 gay and lesbian equal rights march.

According to Dellassandro, each of the incidents helped cause scenes that no American carrier wants to have to deal with. "But in the case of American Airlines, they were very very quickly dealt with. One flight attendant out of a hundred thousand made a bad call, a silly bad call—which got leaked to the press—which is very interesting, but within forty-eight hours Mr. Crandall (the president) himself sent a letter to all employees."

▼ ▼

The letter Dellassandro mentions, one of the most responsibly administered corporate public relations moves on behalf of any American company, stands as an example of how companies should respond when such challenges befall them.

Mr. Crandall wrote, on April 29, 1993:

> We have an aggressive policy of non-discrimination against any individual or group of individuals, and this policy explicitly forbids discrimination for reasons of sexual preference. This policy is especially appropriate for American because we have one of the most diverse work groups in America. . . .
>
> American Airlines apologizes to anyone who was offended by the unfortunate actions of the few employees involved in this unhappy incident. Their actions do not reflect American Airlines' policy or practice, and everyone has my pledge that we will do everything possible to ensure such lapses in judgment do not occur in the future.

Airlines are not the only travel industry taking the lead in gay and lesbian market segments. In 1993 Avis and in 1994 National car rental both officially began waiving the additional driver fee for the partners of their gay and lesbian customers.

According to David Alport, who with Billy Kolber publishes *Out and About,* a gay and lesbian travel newsletter with a subscriber base of 9,500—a readership of at least 15,000 monthly: "We absolutely see all car rental companies moving toward this policy, basically because it makes sense. And this has come about because gay and lesbian consumers pushed for [it]. It's really a fairness issue. The important fact is, that it was the right thing to do."

However, according to Kolber, "Hertz has been fairly adamant in resisting this change. They claim it's a question of insurance liability and loss. I think it's a party line. . . . But at Avis, which went through an employee buyout, they've become much more sensitive to customer issues.

"I predict Hertz will come around in the next few years. There is no way they can't."

David Alport says,

> *I think on the car rental issue we haven't been anywhere near as vocal as we have been on the airline issue. . . . But we are [planning] more editorial coverage in this area which will generate press. And now with two of the four*

▼ ▼

companies having waived their policies, I think it's just going to take a push to drive the other two to follow.

Out and About *recently gave Avis an Editor's Choice award based on their policy changes.*

Fund-raising

Millions of dollars could be raised by some of America's largest and most important nonprofit organizations simply by targeting a portion of their direct-mail and telemarketing fund-raising efforts toward gay and lesbian consumers. In New York, for instance, the United Jewish Appeal Federation is comprised of over literally dozens of different fund-raising divisions—each with a specific focus aimed at donors and potential donors by category. There is a Wall Street division, the women's campaign, a separate campaign for doctors, one for lawyers—even one for the automotive industry, but not one for gay and lesbian contributors. Of course, not all American philanthropic organizations are as large or as well funded as the UJA. But many would benefit from purchasing and at least testing gay and lesbian mailing lists—many of which are now available from or through direct-marketing brokers and gay and lesbian marketing firms.

In the United States today, there are hundreds of nonprofit and not-for-profit gay and lesbian organizations representing tens of millions of dollars in grants, contributions, and in-kind services each year. Interestingly, though, as cautious and organized as gay and lesbian consumers are, there is still no single, officially recognized national gay/lesbian watchdog group currently monitoring the affairs of gay and lesbian nonprofit organizations, other than their own boards and state reporting agencies.

In some cases, in New York City for example, the annual reports of nonprofit groups are not made available to contributors (requiring the donor to write the state for a report), nor are many of these organizations held to any rigorous standard of accountability for their spending by the national gay and lesbian press.

The Wall Street Project, made up of lesbian and gay shareholder activists, could conceivably rise to this role—but vice chair Dianne Bratcher believes that the responsibility for maintaining financial accountability resides within nonprofit and not-for-profit boards and among their donors. Ms. Bratcher, who is also the director of communications for the Interfaith Center on Corporate Responsibility, an association of religous institutional investors active as shareholders around social and environmental issues, comments, "While it may seem that some gay and lesbian not-for-profit groups are not accountable enough, I don't really think that they are really any different from any other not-for-profit groups in the country—except perhaps that they have less money. People have to get involved if they want to hold groups more accountable. It's certainly not an area I think we want government involved in."

To mitigate against even a question of impropriety or mismanagement, gay and lesbian nonprofit organizations (and those with significant gay and lesbian support) should all make their annual financial summaries available upon request. None should require donors or reporters to have to write their state government agencies to obtain records. Especially since state record requirements are highly generalized and rarely broken down beyond program expenses in a way citizens can easily identify how the money was allocated locally. In New York State, for instance, specific allocations by project or department are not required by law to be listed. Moreover, merely being a gay or lesbian organization run by gay people does not mean that such an institution might not fall prey to scandal at some time in the future.

As mainstream for-profit, not-for-profit, and civic organizations continue to move toward more inclusivity in marketing and fundraising efforts, it can be expected they will eventually become more generous in granting and allocating funds and services to gay and lesbian civic, cultural, and philanthropic causes beyond AIDS.

At the present time, as a political safety measure (and moral imperative) the gay and lesbian community should insist that more accountability within its own organizations be adhered to where needed, and that the gay and lesbian press become more active in its monitoring of the gay and lesbian nonprofit community in what is sure to become an evolving and more intimate relationship with corporate America. At minimum, no gay or lesbian nonprofit organization should be allowed to shrink from publishing an annual analysis of its financial activity—and it should make that report easily accessible to the public without cumbersome bureaucratic procedures.

▼ ▼

Gay and Lesbian Book, Magazine, and Newspaper Publishing

Publishing is one of the largest growth industries in the entire gay and lesbian market spectrum. It has long played a role in the development of gay and lesbian local area economies, creating a rallying and source point for gay and lesbian businesses, consumers, readers, and community leaders to organize, communicate, reflect on political ideas, and exchange monies for goods and services.

The sexual revolution of gay men clearly played an economic role in the establishment and growth of gay and lesbian newspapers. The earliest roots of American gay news publishing, dating back to Harlem and the 1920s, are embedded in the historical actions of a few courageous individuals.

In an interview with one of the most important veteran gay activists, Mr. Harry Hay (who many regard as the father of gay liberation), he explained what got the gay and lesbian press going as an economically viable industry (about the late 1950s). It involved the case of *One*, a gay magazine that had been confiscated by the Los Angeles Post Office as obscene because of its mere discussion of homosexuality. Mr. Hay recalls:

> *I suppose that undoubtedly the most major economic impact was our Supreme Court case, because that case opened up all these public uses of the mails. This took us four years and several different [fights in court] to achieve that. But once that was achieved, virtually anything could be sent through the mail. Up until that time, the court had held that as an unstated policy, that the subject could only be 'discussed' in a medical, psychological or religious point of view. You simply could not have a general discussion of homosexuality in a publicly printed piece going through the mail.*
>
> *That was* One *vs.* Olson. *Olson was the Postmaster of L.A. who stopped our mail. We hauled him into court and charged him with violation of federal law. Our attorney was just a young law school graduate, hardly known, but then his phone started ringing from all over the country—Eric Julber. We made our point with a bang. And it automatically legislated for everyone in the then forty-eight states, our decision became the law, and no matter what anybody or any church thought, it is probably the most important civil rights case in our movement that has happened to date.*

From that time forward, more and more individuals began mailing information, newsletters, and booklets through the mails discussing issues of importance to lesbians and gay men. Politics, sex, photographs, and various depictions of nudity in association with editorial copy were incorporated into publications and distributed through the mails. Eventually the distribution channels were extended to adult books and then to major newsstands with the help of *The Advocate* in the late 1970s.

Prior to 1990, every nationally distributed gay or lesbian publication in the United States was economically forced to accept some kind of sexually oriented advertising in order to meet its business expenses. This was the kind of advertising that was used as an excuse by mainstream advertisers as a reason for not advertising. Whether it was phone sex, bathhouse, or personal classified advertisements, it all was seen as inappropriate for the vast majority of display advertisers that had considered the gay and lesbian marketplace at one time or another.

Michael Gravois of Rivendell Marketing says that the number of gay and lesbian publications today that accept sexually oriented advertising is "constantly changing and evolving," but about 15 percent of the publications he represents do not accept any sexually oriented advertising. The reasons informing that policy are all different, based on the local economic climate, editorial policies, etc.

Gravois comments, "Today there are industries being tapped that were untouchable before. There was probably a time when sexually oriented advertising represented a larger portion of our overall billings—1988 to 1990, fifty percent of our billings were related to erotic-oriented advertising, today more like thirty percent."

Today the gay and lesbian press is faced with playing a role that is much different from the early days of activism. As Bob Craig, publisher of *Frontiers* in Southern California, writes:

> As the quantity of news and the importance of gay and AIDS issues has grown, so has the coverage of news in major daily newspapers and the electronic media. As this has occurred, our responsibility as advocacy press has changed significantly. With more gay and AIDS news than anyone can print, our role now is to assess its significance and present that news in a short, concise and unbiased manner—so [our readers] can make informed decisions.[2]

Deacon McCubbin, owner of the Lambda Rising bookstore in Washington D.C., offers a comprehensive direct-mail list totaling

▼ ▼

over 1,600 regularly produced gay and lesbian publications around the world. This list has a combined readership of 16 million gay and lesbian consumers, according to McCubbin. About 300 publications are advertising-supported periodicals serving regional areas of the United States and Canada. In some American cities, there are more weekly gay and lesbian newspapers than there are mainstream news dailies.

In a mail-out research survey conducted for this book of the 150 largest gay and lesbian news publications in the United States (response rate was 62 percent), the most common source of advertising revenue among gay and lesbian news came from independently owned bars, cabarets, restaurants, and discos. The second most common form of advertising was placed by local area professional service firms, such as attorneys, doctors, accountants, florists, carpet cleaning services, etc.

The greatest amount of gay and lesbian publications began to appear in the late 1970s and early 1980s. However, at the national level, prior to 1989, there was not a single, nationally distributed publication with the words *gay* and *lesbian* on the cover—except the bold, controversial *Outweek*. Not even *The Advocate* called itself a gay *and lesbian* publication until pivotal installation of Richard Rouilard as editor-in-chief (1990), whose stewardship alone may have been brought about in part as a reaction to the ever more competitive nature of *Outweek*.

Outweek was America's first nationally distributed gay and lesbian news weekly—a publication with women and people of color listed on its masthead, placed on its covers, and discussed between the covers more than any other publication of its kind. The magazine changed gay and lesbian news publishing in the United States forever. It shook up the New York editorial establishment and the entire gay and lesbian magazine wholesaling industry nationwide. Since that time, a host of other gay and lesbian titles have appeared on the market.

In the words of former editor-in-chief Gabriel Rotello, "*Outweek* magazine provided a forum that helped to shape and crystalize the moment, for AIDS, for activism, and for a new generation of activists."

Former *Outweek* columnist Michaelangelo Signorile says:

> Outweek *magazine put so many issues on the front burner for the first time, so many issues that had not been discussed before—*Outweek *encouraged dis-*

▼ ▼

cussion, it pushed all issues out front, whether it was AIDS, health care, government, or outing. Outweek *got the media to focus so much on gay and lesbian issues, it really was the voice of a new generation, a voice that was much more vocal, one that wasn't going to allow the media to keep [public figures] invisible.*

When asked about outing, Signorile said:

The word outing *was something created by* Time *magazine, the word does a disservice to what we are talking about. We are talking about equalizing, whenever sexuality is relevant, it should be discussed. The same goes for homosexuality. It should be free to be discussed just like heterosexuality. People in America know everything about every public figure—do they have a husband, a wife, children? We know that information when it comes to heterosexual public figures. Outing is simply about saying that there are times when homosexuality is very much about what an individual is saying—when they are an elected public official. In that regard [*Outweek*] really did change much of the media. In fact, the media today has moved dramatically on this issue, we see a discussion of sexuality when it's relevant. . . . We now see public figures being asked if they are gay or lesbian.*

Indeed, since *Outweek,* even the *New York Times* has commented on public officials that have been pressed on the issue of their sexual orientation. *The Advocate* outed former Pentagon spokesperson Pete Williams, which helped fuel the debate over gays and lesbians in the U.S. military and the *Wall Street Journal* published a front-page story on publisher Jann Wenner of *Rolling Stone,* citing romantic changes in his personal life and their relation to his business affairs.

Prior to 1994, much of the tabloid press participated in outing a slew of Hollywood public figures, and newspapers began debating whether or not it was ethical to print the names of rape victims during prominent public trials. This new openness was fueled in part by *Outweek* magazine.

Perhaps *Outweek*'s most controversial moment occurred when Malcolm Forbes died. *Outweek* was the only publication to print an honest story about the man's life, and the story was promoted like crazy (it was actually mailed to every major television newsroom affiliate in the United States, creating an instantaneous media sensation). With the Malcolm Forbes story, newsstand circulation orders grew dramatically. Suddenly bookstore chains were willing

▼ ▼

to distribute the magazine. Days earlier they weren't returning phone calls.

Money talks. A little hype doesn't hurt. More times than not it really helps. But all hype is nothing. *Outweek* had substance, spirit, and character. It made people think. It made America talk and take positions.

Outweek magazine was revolutionary in other ways. Its experiment with the removal of sexually oriented advertising raised eyebrows on Madison Avenue. This heightened the sensitivity and appeal of other publications, including *Genre,* which—like *Out*—was success-fully launched nationwide without any sexually oriented advertising and is still publishing today.

Since that time numerous efforts have been made to launch a publication in the New York City area for gay and lesbian con-sumers—a city with a completely different, much more complex gay and lesbian economy. New York writer Mark Schoofs attempted to start a newspaper for gays and lesbians in New York, but after much research came to the conclusion that it was, at least for him, not possible at the time.

Schoofs comments, "Newspapers in general are risky to invest in. Asking people to invest a sizable amount of money with the econ-omy in bad shape—it was asking too much. We were able to raise forty percent of what we need, we raised $400,000. We were trying to raise a million."

Since that time *LGNY* (*Lesbian and Gay New York*) was launched early in 1995 by former *QW* publisher (and *Outweek* advertising exec-utive) Troy Masters. The publication deserves the support of the New York gay and lesbian business community, and only time will tell if it can find a voice and establish itself more firmly and with more longevity than its spirited and much missed predecessors.

Today there are more national gay and lesbian magazine publica-tions in the United States than at any other time in history—tucked into newsstands and drugstore shelves and rural shopping mall bookstores in Idaho. Almost as common as apple pie. But long before news publishing, the gay and lesbian market was setting down historical roots.

Since Radcliffe Hall's controversial *The Well of Loneliness* in 1928, an entire generation of gay and lesbian readers has passed through the world without ever experiencing the feeling of walking into a bookstore designed especially for them. Today there is a gay or les-

▼ ▼

bian bookstore in nearly every major American city in the United States. Literally hundreds of bookstores now stock gay and lesbian titles under the specific heading of Gay and Lesbian Studies.

Gay and lesbian book publishing was extremely important to the lesbian movement. Barbara Grier, publisher of Nyad Press, remembers the days back in the 1950s when she was editing *The Ladder* for the Daughters of Bilitis—a pioneering organization for lesbians in America. "We mimeographed it in the basement of Macy's on company time."

Today Ms. Grier's successful Nyad Press grosses in excess of $1.5 million annually and is currently paying out royalties to over one hundred writers each year.

In the 1950s and 1960s, hundreds and hundreds of lesbian-themed paperback novels were published—many of which were written by men for the erotic enjoyment of other men. As it turned out, many lesbians were attracted to the books and a literal revolution in lesbian political communication grew out of the phenomenon. This dynamic, combined with the women's underground music movement in the 1970s, had a strong economic affect on the ability of women to organize and share political ideas, emotions, and friendship through written words and lyrics.

In November 1967, the Oscar Wilde Bookstore opened in New York City. It was the first bookstore of its kind, stocked primarily with gay/lesbian-themed literature, nonfiction, newspapers, and magazines. Bill Offenbaker, the former owner, says that sales have predominantly been fiction—about 75 percent—and 25 percent for nonfiction. "Women tend to buy more paperback murder mysteries; men tend to buy the hardcovers, both fiction and nonfiction." The bookstore, which currently stocks over 10,000 titles, saw an increase in the sales of relationship books among men in the past few years. "It happens every year in spring," Offenbaker says.

In 1979, A Different Light Bookstore opened on the West Coast in the Silverlake section of Los Angeles. A Different Light eventually opened stores in New York in 1983, in San Francisco in 1986, and in 1990 moved its Silverlake store to West Hollywood. Recently A Different Light moved from its Greenwich Village location to the growing Chelsea area of Manhattan. Owner Norman Laurila and general manager Roz Parr said that business had grown in the New York store by so much, that on weekends you could hardly move inside it. Their new store has four times the amount of room.

▼ ▼

A Different Light's growth is a particularly telling commentary on the extraordinary growth of the gay and lesbian book publishing industry—most of which occurred in the 1980s.

A hallmark of A Different Light is the fact that they keep nearly every gay and lesbian book in print stocked in their stores—currently over 15,000 titles. Roz Parr believes that the combined inventory of gay and lesbian–themed books in A Different Light and books of gay and lesbian interest could possibly approach 25,000 by the year 2000.

Most gay and lesbian bookstores report that 70 to 85 percent of their sales are in books, with the remainder composed of magazines, newspapers, and journals. (Of those stores carrying erotic magazines, many bookstore managers that were contacted claimed at least 50 percent of their magazine sales to be in the erotic category and predominantly male-oriented.)

Jed Mattes, a literary agent since 1975 for a wide range of authors, including the late Vito Russo of *The Celluloid Closet*, believes the market will continue to grow, but will become more and more diversified. Discussions with other book editors and publishing agents in New York reveal parallel thinking regarding the future of the gay and lesbian publishing market.

Mattes comments, "There are certain [publishing] houses that are more likely than others to [publish a gay or lesbian book] but I don't think there is one house that I would say, no don't send it to them, they won't buy. There are some houses that are unlikely, but not because they are hostile. I think some houses just don't have a sales force that is as knowledgeable as some others, or they don't have editors that are [thinking in those terms]."

Deacon McCubbin of the Lambda Rising Bookstore in Washington believes he could easily have a total stock of over 20,000 different gay and lesbian titles by the year 2000. He predicts this "in large part because there are so many more gay people coming out, and more and more straight people interested in gay-themed books—especially straight people who work with gay people, which is an increasingly large number of people all the time. We have always had a substantial straight clientele since we opened in 1974."

McCubbin says he expects Lambda Rising to gross over $3.8 million by the end of 1995. That is not hard to believe, considering the

▼ ▼

Lambda Rising Bookstore probably has the most well-guarded mailing list in the entire gay and lesbian retail marketplace—over 60,000 names. The list is not for sale or for rent (although joint campaigns—riders—have been known to happen). Interestingly, Lambda Rising's best mail-order customers are in Texas and Florida.

Currently there are over 140 gay and lesbian bookstores in the United States, 145 lesbian feminist bookstores, and probably over 500 general interest bookstores with gay and lesbian book sections (a trend that has developed over the last ten years). The market's future appears to be heading in a direction of continued growth and diversification, with books focusing on political organizing, community analysis, and changing gay and lesbian culture. A key theme surrounds individual gays and lesbians needing to become more involved in their own gay and lesbian communities—many want to know how they can become more a part of the overall gay and lesbian community.

A number of bookstore managers say gay and lesbian customers have a strong need to know what's happening in the national community and how one can get involved in empowering the national gay and lesbian political process.

The exploding gay and lesbian publishing world is allowing a new generation of gays and lesbians to celebrate their sexuality and spirit—especially in areas of the country where gay and lesbian culture is not as defined, open, and progressive. Trends over the next few years in gay and lesbian book sales will undoubtedly reflect changes in gay and lesbian culture. In the late 1970s and early 1980s sales agents complained they couldn't get retail bookstores to stock gay and lesbian titles. Times have clearly changed.

Media, Advertising, and Direct Marketing

An entire sourcebook could be written on the gay and lesbian media and advertising business alone. Every major American city now has a least one firm specializing in some kind of gay and lesbian marketplace-oriented activity for businesses in search of advice, public relations assistance, or complete advertising campaigns down to the media placement.

▼ ▼

Rather than attempting to catalogue what is now easily more than twenty-five sizable gay and lesbian marketing, advertising, and public relations specialty firms nationwide, who their clients are, and what their professional relationships are becoming within the emerging gay and lesbian media business, I've opted instead to include a sampling of a variety of campaigns (see insert) that have been launched over the past couple of years. In addition, there is a listing of important gay and lesbian business and consumer organizations in Appendix A that can be consulted for more information regarding gay/lesbian-owned firms.

A sampling of what some of America's more involved and out gay and lesbian market pioneers are thinking is worth mentioning, as are a few remarks and insights I recorded in interviews with key gay and lesbian marketplace thinkers.

Two advertising industry professionals active within the gay and lesbian community and on staff at two of the most important agencies on Madison Avenue are Mark Horn, a senior copywriter and vice president with Wunderman Cato Johnson, a Young and Rubicam direct-marketing agency, and Nancy Webster, a creative director at Burson Marsteller. Both individuals are members of the New York Advertising and Communications Network, one of the country's largest gay and lesbian professional organizations.[3]

In a joint interview with Ms. Webster and Mr. Horn, interesting insights emerged surrounding each of their takes on the shrewdness of IKEA's recent foray into gay and lesbian target marketing, a television commercial of a gay male couple buying home furnishings.

"I was shocked at the IKEA ad," intoned Mr. Horn. "They spent money [targeting] the community and it got out in the world-at-large in a way that had a political effect that all my years of political activism never had. Although, years of activism may ultimately have led IKEA to do it. But [that combination] in its own way is very important, very supportive. I will always give money and my business to people who support me, I will certainly not give my money to Cracker Barrel restaurants[4] or to people who want to burn me at the stake."

The advertisement no doubt broke new ground and earned IKEA much publicity and an award from GLAAD, but some gay and lesbian marketing professionals noted that the advertisement showed only men, which surely had to annoy more than a few les-

▼ ▼

bian shoppers. Especially since there's no definitive data that lesbians buy fewer mid-priced dining tables than gay men do.

Nancy Webster perceived the IKEA advertising as a shrewd and insightful example illustrative of how much advertising relies on sending a variety of messages to a variety of different consumer groups commenting, "'Gay' connotes men, you use the word gay, so you're talking about men. It's almost easier for women to pass, you have less of an idea of difference. One of the reasons that some gay women are not out at work is because they really can pass more easily than gay men. If a woman is living alone or with a family member, nobody thinks that much about that, but if it's an older man living with his brother, people think about it and wonder. It goes back to this idea of difference—two women shopping together is typical, two men shopping together is different.

"It's been my experience that many heterosexual women love gay men. I think that straight women love gay men more than they love lesbians. I don't think they have a problem with lesbians, but I think that IKEA was thinking about straight women.

"Advertising reduces people to markets and people in advertising to objects," acknowledges Horn. "And in as much as gay people are becoming more a part of society, gay culture and gay men and women are experiencing equal opportunity exploitation. It will be interesting to see how lesbians do or do not become objectified in advertising in years to come."

Gay and Lesbian Direct Marketing Lists

By far, the best list rentals available for self-identifying gay and lesbian consumers comes from the Strubco Company in New York, regional gay and lesbian news publications and subscription services, a few regional gay and lesbian bookstores, national glossy magazines, private membership clubs, some nonprofit groups, and, increasingly, gay/lesbian-owned retail businesses.

Using direct marketing as a way of reaching the gay and lesbian market is not only effective, but it's a smart way to test the waters for companies who are considering marketing to gays and lesbians for the first time.

The use of direct marketing to gays and lesbians also allows for more disclosure in language and imagery—language and imagery that some marketers may fear incorporating into a magazine or

▼ ▼

outdoor advertising vehicle. The direct-marketing examples shown in the photo insert illustrate the varying approaches that have been applied to direct-marketing efforts for different gay and lesbian market segments.

Direct marketing also provides the comfort (although in a somewhat illusory way) for marketers of appearing to be risk-free in terms of profile: the magazine is kept longer by the consumer; direct mail gets thrown away by those who don't intend to take advantage of it. It's a low-profile, highly targeted medium allowing versatility in segmentation and an excellent opportunity for a company to begin building its own gay and lesbian customer database.

Among lists available from Strubco, there are interests and activities among gay and lesbian donor and prospect names that may be of particular interest to marketers in the following areas:

Art/Antique Collecting
Cultural/Art Events
Donating and Volunteering to Charitable Groups
Foreign Travel
Gourmet Cooking/Fine Foods
Owning a CD Player
Personal Home Computing
Physical Fitness, Sports, and Exercise Activities
Buying CDs or Tapes
Fine Wines

Shocking Gray founders Cindy Cesnalis, David Owen, and Michelle Friesenhahn launched one of the first gay and lesbian direct-mail catalogs in June of 1991. According to Ms. Cesnalis, they turned a sizable profit within the second year, which is extraordinary considering that most direct-mail start-ups don't reach solvency for at least five years.

Ms. Cesnalis claims their success was in part due to the highly responsive nature of the gay and lesbian home-shopping market. Rick Hutcheson, Shocking Gray's president and CEO, says products today range in price from $20 to $80. Originally the price spread was from as little as $3.99 for jewelry and cards to as high as $1,200 for a premium designer mirror product.

Cenalis comments, "Anything that's pride-related sells very well, including luggage, checkbook covers with pink triangles, rainbow flags, etc." (Which may be true for Shocking Gray since the "rainbow look" has been part of their image, but pink triangles and rainbows are starting to bore many gay and lesbian consumers in the larger gay and lesbian urban enclaves.)

Shocking Gray started with a small list purchased through Strubco that has grown to 130,000 strong. Other companies who have rented the Shocking Gray list claim response rates as high as 3 percent compared with average industry reponse rates, but Shocking Gray has seen responses as high as 8 percent on some of its own mailings.

Two other successful direct-marketing offshoots from Shocking Gray include their highly stylized M2M catalog aimed exclusively at gay men, and the Best Sellers Club catalog. Shocking Gray's only competition for the longest time seemed to be other start-ups, which disappeared as fast as they appeared. But that is changing as other successful companies, such as Don't Panic, and direct-mail products offered through gay and lesbian publications like *Deneuve* and *The Advocate* stake out their own direct-marketing turf.

Yet Shocking Gray's success underscores once again the importance of being perceived as not only first, but as a consistent, dependable product or service leader within the gay and lesbian community.

Gay/lesbian-owned ad agencies, or agencies specializing in gay and lesbian advertising and media, are growing rapidly across the United States as well. This trend can be expected to continue over the next ten years as more and more gay and lesbian markets diversify and start requiring more specialized service providers in gay and lesbian regional markets.

More small firms are now becoming full-scale advertising agencies as specialization becomes the trend in travel promotion and management, the affinity credit card business, long-distance telephone communications, and niche market research and focus group management. Larger agencies are also now making their foray into the marketplace, such as Hill & Knowlton; Bragman, Nyman, Caferelli; and, of course, Yankelovich Partners.

Staying Informed About Gay and Lesbian Markets

Gay and lesbian market segments are emerging so fast—both domestically and abroad—that magazines, newspapers, and newsletters are being launched just to cover the news.

▼ ▼

For a noncommercially supported source of gay and lesbian market news, refer to *Quotient* newsletter produced by Dan Baker, Harold Levine, and Sean Strub in New York City. Individuals wishing to stay abreast of gay and lesbian entrepreneur activity will want to subscribe to *Victory*, out of San Francisco, which follows gay and lesbian market issues and news but focuses more closely on the aspects related to gay and lesbian market investment, management, and business-to-business relationships. Other useful reference sources on gay and lesbian advertising, business, and marketing trends can be obtained through *Next News*, published by George Sancoucy out of New York, an advertiser-supported glossy; and *Out and About,* a noncommercial travel newsletter aimed at gay and lesbian travelers that is followed closely by gay and lesbian travel industry professionals.

It should also be noted that some gay and lesbian regional news publications also do an excellent job of covering gay and lesbian market news, as do the Gay Cable Network, run by Lou Maletta, and Gay Entertainment Television, run by Marvin Schwamm, both in New York City. Marketers should also consider contacting the New York Advertising and Communications Network (see Appendix A).

Any company hoping to keep up on gay and lesbian market segments would be wise to contact one or more of these publications or organizations since industry trade publications do not as yet track gay and lesbian spending on a regular basis.

Emerging Market Dynamics

Nearly any American company manufacturing, selling, or marketing products to consumers—particularly in heavily populated areas—can benefit from positioning its products to gay and lesbian Americans. Not all products need to be directly positioned through gay and lesbian media, but few can cite evidence that they are actually reaching gay and lesbian consumers via the mainstream exclusively. This is particularly apparent in Detroit's willingness to begin targeting gay and lesbian consumers through gay media in the marketing of automobiles. Because the fact is that spectacular opportunities really do exist for automobile sales as well as products, parts, and service maintenance companies among gays and lesbians. Nearly every gay or lesbian consumer in the United States who has a driver's license (with the exception of New York City) drives an automobile.

▼ ▼

Considering how loyal gays and lesbians can be, there would be no easier way to immediately increase domestic car sales—even more than the record numbers posted in 1994—than for the Big Three automakers to target a slice of their advertising toward the gay and lesbian consumer automotive markets.

While numerous dealerships have successfully advertised to gay men and lesbians through regional publications, it took the Swedish manufacturer Saab to take the plunge, targeting gay and lesbian Americans through the pages of gay and lesbian publications.

While it is clear that the music industry, fashion merchandising aimed at both gay men and lesbians, small businesses, small business franchising, computer hardware and software marketing, and individual psychotherapy and other mental and physical health care industries are now targeting this demographic, only those companies that either place ads in gay and lesbian publications or take the strategic information contained in this book and in other references to heart when producing their overall advertising campaigns for the mainstream will be the ones that establish long-term relationships with gay and lesbian consumers.

This is, perhaps, nowhere more apparent than in the rapidly changing field of American medicine. "Any pharmaceutical or biotech company investing money in AIDS research now views [meeting with the consumer] as a must," according to David Gold, a writer and former director of the medical information program at GMHC (Gay Men's Health Crisis) in New York City, the nation's oldest and largest AIDS service organization. Mr. Gold states that:

> . . . *as soon as AIDS began impacting people lives—around the mid 1980s— the stakes were so high that gays and lesbians—but predominantly gay men— started creating huge organizations in their communities. First you had big social service industries developing within the gay community, which had never happened before. Then you had gay people learning everything about the pharmaceutical industry—which eventually changed patient care across the country. Now we have openly gay patient care advocates at the highest levels of the medical establishment [in the United States]. Now you see major businesses targeting people with AIDS or HIV. It has come full circle with companies now viewing gays in the medical fields as important and informed consumers.*

▼ ▼

In the beginning these companies did not want to have anything to do with activists, then ACT-UP (AIDS Coalition to Unleash Power) got into the head-quarters of Burroughs Wellcome and barricaded themselves in their offices until they would listen.

Today medical companies actively pursue these activists. Companies now fly me and [other activists] out to their headquarters to see if we think the drug approval process is coming along properly. We basically now [strategize together and share information] to get drugs approved more rapidly.

You now see this [phenomenon developing] with breast cancer and prostate cancer advocacy groups. And these [new activists are taking their cues] by virtue of what they witnessed happening with AIDS activism in the gay community.

I don't think it would be an understatement at all to say that the way the gay community has dealt with AIDS has transformed the American health care industry. The doctor-patient relationship has been forever altered. In many cases, AIDS and cancer patients now know more than the doctors—that has never happened in the history of medicine.

David Gold's words should be heeded by large companies that hope to sell products and services to gays and lesbians. While it is true that AIDS activism bears the reality and urgency of life and death and time's passage through history, as we approach the next presidential election and numerous Supreme Court decisions affecting gay and lesbian Americans as well as heterosexual Americans, more tension builds among gay and lesbian consumer enclaves across the United States—both within and outside of large corporate establishments.

Gay and lesbian consumers are simply going to continue to flex their financial and organizational muscle. And business can only profit by incorporating them into the process—as an ally—in much the same way the medical field has had to learn to do.

In addition, it should be kept in mind that if gay and lesbian Americans are able to influence the nation's health care industry and the military establishment, if they are winning the attention of American automakers, then it is only a matter of time before their impact becomes more closely associated with smaller and more mid-sized companies as well as the major political parties and influ-ential lobbying groups.

As the global economy expands, more will surely be revealed about how all Americans will begin to approach the business of *con-ducting business* in the domestic consumer marketplace.

▼ ▼

If modern medicine is any indicator, profitable businesses can no longer afford to ignore the trend toward making gay and lesbian—and eventually all heterosexual—Americans more a part of the overall, socially evolving producer to consumer processes. Because their ability to compete and post profits in the coming days will simply depend on these new emerging market dynamics.

▼ ▼

CHAPTER 7

THE FUTURE OF THE GAY AND LESBIAN MARKETPLACE

Considerations at the Door of the Twenty-first Century

The athletes came from all over the world—10,000 of them, from 40 different countries—all to compete in 31 different sporting events. They came from Europe, from Africa, from South America, Japan, and Canada. There were men and women, people with disabilities, teenagers, parents, war veterans, business owners, government employees, actors and actresses, Olympic Gold Medalists, even the Republican mayor of New York City. And when Patti LaBelle sang "Somewhere Over the Rainbow" in Yankee Stadium, there was a moment when everyone felt the pull of history wrap around their shoulders. It was a pull that took everyone back to their childhood—back to the yellow brick road and the feeling of home.

It was warm, validating—as American as it gets.

"Gay Games won't be ignored," chimed *Advertising Age*[1] more than five months prior to the historical adventure. And indeed they weren't. Just weeks later the *New York Times* reported that the city's Civilian Complaint Review Board member Reverend Ruben Diaz (a sort of Gay Games Scrooge in the days preceding the event) wrote a column appearing in several Spanish-language newspapers claiming that the Games would lead the young "to conclude that if there are so many gay and lesbian athletes, then there is nothing wrong . . . " He was absolutely right.

A line that ran in a *Wall Street Journal* article just prior to the games (which coincided with the twenty-fifth anniversary of the Stonewall Riots)[2] summed up the gay and lesbian community's march through history quite well: "The times they certainly are a'changing." A headline that appeared in the New York *Daily News* shortly after the Stonewall Riot in 1969, "Homo Nest Raided. Queen Bees Are Sting Mad," would be inconceivable today.

As more sensitivity takes hold, marketing experts are beginning to see what little risk there really is for companies to align themselves with an event that caters to what used to be called an "alternative lifestyle."

That reality was echoed by Doug Alligood, vice president of special markets at BBDO, New York, who was quoted in the *New York Times* in an early piece about the Gay Games: "We know all the negatives haven't melted away. People say, 'I have the right to spend my money the way I want,' and it's hard to argue with that."[3]

Indeed, even a full year prior to the Games sell-out crowd in Yankee Stadium, high-profile advertisements appeared throughout the New York City subway system pitching tolerance and understanding of a people whose time has finally come. The campaign's creative development was a pro bono effort sponsored by the Gay and Lesbian Alliance Against Defamation (GLAAD). It featured people from all walks of life, including a clergyman with his gay son, former gay and lesbian community liaison Dr. Marjorie Hill, Manhattan restaurant owner Florent Morellet, and even a direct-mail marketer and popular entertainment fund-raiser dressed as a female impersonator, Charles Ching, a.k.a. Coco LaChine. Nothing was hidden, it was all very matter-of-fact.

The *Times* couldn't help but notice that moment as well: "Each person is photographed next to an assertive or personal statement. For instance, Florent Morellet, owner of Florent, a restaurant in Manhattan, says, 'I think it's essential that we respect each other's right to do as we like with our minds, our bodies and our lives.'"[4] GLAAD executive director (at that time) Ellen Carton said, "Given the purpose of the campaign, it was important that real people be shown in the ads, rather than models or representations of gay men and lesbians."

▼ ▼

The times in fact are a'changing. History will recall the end of this century as the turning point in gay and lesbian emancipation in America. It will also recall the last half of the century as the golden years of American gay and lesbian cultural visibility—a time for gay and lesbian people that was filled with promise, progress, and economic momentum. Social legitimacy and equal status finally arrived for themselves and their families as a long-ignored but important minority of people—a people intricately woven into the spiritual fabric of the nation.

But history will also underline those who stood in Gay and Lesbian America's way—who refused to support basic traditional American values. It will record the never-ending grief, shame, castigation, and hypocrisy surrounding AIDS, AIDS funding, and AIDS education that various people and organizations within American culture sought to scapegoat. It will heap scorn on the political extremists who sought to extinguish the cultural lifeblood of a part of America that has always been undeniable. And in time, these facts and more will make their way into our children's history books—in the same way the history of slavery, worldwide multiculturalism, the extermination of Jews, and the systematic repression of American women's rights have.

As American gay and lesbian culture expands, it also becomes more fragmented. Yet it is stronger because of that fragmentation.

As my friend Alan Roskoff, assistant to New York Public Advocate Mark Greene, commented, "I meet people who are openly gay and assume that we have a lot in common politically and then I find out they are gay Republicans. . . . Twenty years ago when I met people active in the gay movement, they were antiwar activists by and large, not people I would find myself on opposite sides of the aisle with arguing over economic issues or race relations."

As surprised as Alan may often find himself in comparison to days gone by, his observation is right on target. As the Yankelovich data in this book illustrates, gay and lesbian individuals are in fact as much like the rest of America as they are not. They are not all of a single mindset. They are Republican and Democrat. They are single and in committed relationships. They have children, they own homes, they make investments, and they are informed. They do not necessarily all think alike—nor do they advocate the same political agenda for each other, even though they may have a more liberal perspective on freedom. But many of their ideas are parallel with

▼ ▼

the majority of Americans when it comes to education, civic responsibility, spiritually morality, strong family ties, economic thrift, and individual opportunity.

Today gay and lesbian people's status within American culture may be marked by constitutional and legal uncertainty, and numerous political challenges remain. But as the clock ticks louder and louder with the issues surrounding gay and lesbian emancipation at the government level, business will continue to surge ahead.

The movement for equal rights of gay and lesbian Americans is an issue whose time has come. It is a time when we should all be asking ourselves whether or not we are going to allow liberty and democracy to endure and extend to all Americans regardless of age, sex, race, ethnicity, creed, religion, *and sexual orientation,* or if we are going to allow ourselves to put limits on our interpretation of what a free society can be in the twenty-first century.

In order for people to remain free, business must remain free. It must be monitored by reasonable regulation, but at the same time be free to conduct itself in an "enterprising" fashion that recognizes opportunity, growth, and the expansion of markets. Today that includes gay and lesbian consumers. And as more marketing is aimed at gay and lesbian consumers by both large and small businesses, it will become all the more apparent to gay customers that the companies that are not with them may, perhaps, be against them.

The gay and lesbian emancipation movement and the consumer revolution it has inspired is one that has shaken and unveiled the cowardice of the world's toughest generals in the U.S. Department of Defense. It has rattled the Office of the President. It has challenged judges, clergy, police officers, and national spokespeople from Dade County, Florida, to federal marshals on patrol in Mississippi.

It is not going to go away.

In some ways, the legitimacy of one's sexual orientation as a social, political, economic, and spiritual identity is a moot point that can no longer be debated. Because it already exists in reality, at every level of society.

Gay and lesbian sexuality is not a lifestyle. It is a life *fact.*

As the issues surrounding that certitude continue to be fought in city councils, statehouses, and school board meetings across America, some of the brightest hope for change and leadership is coming

▼ ▼

from our corporate boardrooms and marketing planning committees. American business has often moved faster than government.

But that is because a growing business cannot wait. And growing
businesses in America that seek opportunity, expansion, and legiti-
mate new consumer markets that are stable, innovative, and part of
the unfolding panorama of American free enterprise must step up
to the plate like good sportspeople always do—and play ball.

Business can rest assured that it has a friend in gay and lesbian
America. But it must communicate to gay and lesbian consumers
that gay and lesbian consumers have a friend in American business.

The time to take action is now.

America's best businesses will see and take advantage of the
opportunity for change, growth, and social renewal that is related
to their partnering with the gay and lesbian consumer revolution in
America. They will recognize that their profits are no longer
immune from the issues surrounding gay and lesbian freedoms—
both in the courtrooms and the marketplace.

American business does not have to become a forum where gay
and lesbian political battles are fought. And if American business
wants to avoid the coming battles surrounding that debate, it will
side with gay and lesbian people—as individuals, as employees, and
consumers—and as Americans.

Business need only seek to support gay and lesbian individuality
both in its treatment of gay and lesbian labor and in its recognition
of gay and lesbian consumption. The gay and lesbian consumer revolution is born of informed, organized individuals who are realizing that their fight for human rights is now becoming an economic
process as much as it has been a political process—a new cultural
dynamism of identity.

To support equal rights for gay and lesbian Americans is to join
in the ongoing fight for the protection of everyone's individual
rights.

The business leaders who are taking a stand and establishing or
reaffirming their commitment to gay and lesbian emancipation are
taking a stand for their own economic prosperity as well.

You can't have free enterprise without free individuals.

In the final analysis, businesses that support the call for stronger
protection of individual liberties—regardless of sexual orientation—will be the businesses that become leaders among America's
emerging national family of gay and lesbian consumers.

▼ ▼

If business truly believes that ultimately the customer is right—regardless of sexual orientation—then business need only listen, provide the goods, and reap the benefits: a more talented work force, a greater profit margin, and more competitive products and services.

The Gay Games in 1994 made clear to the world that gay and lesbian people are going to go on living their lives, developing their own communities, their own institutions of pride and sustenance.

In a perfect world, there would be no need for a Gay Games, Gay Pride, or even a gay and lesbian marketplace.

But in a perfect world, Brenda and Wanda Henson of Camp Sister Spirit would be able to run their private women's retreat in Mississippi without having to suffer at the hands of bigots and have Attorney General Janet Reno send in federal marshals to bring an end to the crisis of harassment that had befallen their community.

The Hensons would be able to buy gravel and supplies without being faced with restraint of trade issues all across their county. In a perfect world Camp Sister Spirit wouldn't have to fight in court to apply United States Code 241, known as the Anti-Clan Act, to get, as Wanda Henson exclaims in a broken voice, "the neighbors to leave us alone. This is why we need a civil rights law to protect gays and lesbians. I don't mind putting my ass on the line like this but I need help. A cow farmer that was selling hay to [us] was ordered by neighbors to stop. [When he didn't] two of his calves were shot.

"The Justice Department attorneys told us, 'We're sorry but there are no civil rights laws to protect you, none for gays and lesbians. I asked how can this be?"

Now you know why *Victory* magazine gave the Hensons the gay and lesbian Entrepreneurial Award for 1995, because Camp Sister Spirit represents more than homophobia, more than bigotry, it symbolizes the ongoing fight against the unfair economic practices and social policies that are largely unaddressed at this late date in democratic history.

Perhaps Harold Levine, director of marketing for Gay Games 1994 paints the gay and lesbian marketing picture best. He—like I—sees a road filled with hope, headed toward change, prosperity, and goodwill for both American business and gay and lesbian people—as well as straight people everywhere—in his comment:

▼ ▼

In retrospect, the Gay Games marked the point when marketers stopped asking whether they should market to the gay and lesbian community and started asking how they should reach out to this marketplace. Mainstream sponsors reaped enormous benefits from the Games. A mail survey conducted ten weeks after the Games by the Gay Games organizing committee found unaided recall of over 35 percent for Naya Water, Miller Beer, and AT&T, twice what a mainstream event sponsorship could be expected to bring. And the Games also laid to rest widespread fears of a right-wing backlash. Mainstream sponsors were highly visible, and the press covered the involvement of Miller Beer, Continental Airlines, Naya Water, and AT&T in depth. There was no backlash. What sponsors did find was an enormous gratitude among gay men and lesbians—that they had supported an event so important to gay and lesbian people across the United States—in fact, around the world.

And, as America's best businesspeople know, the customer is always right.

APPENDIX A

▼ ▼

INDEPENDENT INFORMATION SOURCES FOR GAY- AND LESBIAN-ORIENTED ADVERTISERS AND MARKETERS

The National Association of People with AIDS
1413 K Street NW, 7th Floor
Washington, D.C. 20005
(202) 898-0414

The National Gay and Lesbian Task Force
2320 17th Street, NW
Washington, D.C. 20009
(202) 332-6483

Council on Economic Priorities
30 Irving Place
New York, NY 10003
(212) 420-1133

The New York Advertising and Communications Network
Box 149
332 Bleeker Street
New York, NY 10014-2980
24-hour message line: (212) 517-0380

▼ ▼

The Gay and Lesbian Alliance Against Defamation
150 West 26th Street #503
New York, NY 10001
(212) 807-1700

The Wall Street Project
185 East 85th Street Suite 25A
New York, NY 10028-2147
(212)870-2296

The Human Rights Campaign Fund
P.O. Box 1396
Washington, D.C. 20013
(202) 628-4160

▼ ▼

A NOTE ON YANKELOVICH MONITOR SENSITIVITY TECHNIQUES

In an effort to provide a broad picture of what is going on in the minds of American consumers, the Yankelovich MONITOR® covers a wide variety of subjects, many of them extremely sensitive. In order to insure accurate information on these issues, Yankelovich has constructed a number of research techniques to alleviate embarrassment or anxiety on the respondent's part.

Two are particularly worth noting again because of their relationship to the gay and lesbian sample participants and those that responded as gay, lesbian, or homosexual:

- The 1.5-hour questionnaire is administered in the respondent's home—a secure environment controlled by the respondent.
- Sensitive topics, such as those dealing with individual identity, are placed in a spiral binder of exhibit cards. For such questions, each respondent is instructed to turn to the appropriate card and asked to indicate only the numbers of the responses they choose. In this way, respondents disclose information confidentially.

Further, each individual is scored based upon responses to a series of questions. Scores are used for two primary reasons:

- Tracking from years past to determine the size and direction of social change
- To compare and contrast two or more groups in order to gain insight into the motivations and needs of one group versus another

▼ ▼

IDENTIFICATION OF A SCIENTIFICALLY RELEVANT GAY/LESBIAN SAMPLE

The highly accurate scientific sample of gay/lesbian respondents identified for this study was obtained by means of an item in the 1993 Yankelovich MONITOR questionnaire that asked participants to choose from a descriptive list of 52 adjectives/phrases those items that describe them. One of the 52 descriptors was "gay/lesbian/homosexual."

The information contained in the following data represents approximately 6 percent of the 2,503 respondents, 16 years of age and older (n=148), who indicated that "gay/lesbian/homosexual" described them. This sophisticated self-identification technique is significantly more reliable than others which have been used to analyze the gay/lesbian population in the past.

Population samples made up of magazine, catalog, and direct-marketing subscription lists—or of those who voluntarily return mail questionnaires—are neither random nor representative of the population as a whole. By their very nature they contain substantial bias because they only represent those consumers. Yet, not in any way does this disparage the value of using information or lists culled from various marketing companies—even if their methods of obtaining names relies heavily on convenience sampling. It is important to know in placing media what a specific magazine's readers are like, or what a specific marketing companies lists or panel of participants is like. But that information is only representative of those publications and marketing company panels, and cannot be accurately extrapolated to the population as a whole.

NOTES

▼ ▼

1: You Can Take It to the Bank

1. See Vito Russo, *The Celluloid Closet* (New York: Harper & Row, 1981, 1987).
2. Randy Shilts, *Conduct Unbecoming: Gays and Lesbians in the U.S. Military* (New York: St. Martin's Press, 1993), p. 15.
3. Roger Ricklefs, *Wall Street Journal,* May 1, 1995. (See Enterprise column.)
4. As of September 1, 1994.
5. Peter Rutten, Albert F. Bayers III, and Kelly Maloni, *Net Guide: Your Map to the Services, Information and Entertainment on the Electronic Highway* (New York: Random House Electronic Publishing, 1994).
6. Cornell West, *Race Matters* (Boston: Beacon Press, 1993), p. 25.
7. Erik Larson, *The Naked Consumer: How Our Private Lives Become Public Commodities* (New York: Henry Holt, 1992), p. 68.
8. Mary L. Roberts and Paul D. Berger, *Direct Marketing Management* (New York: Prentice Hall, 1989) pp. 135, 136.

2: Visibility: The New Politics of Profit

1. Murray Edelman, "The Gay and Lesbian Vote and Estimates of Population Size," prepared for presentation at the annual meeting of the American Statistical Association, August 1994, Toronto, Ontario, Canada. For a complete copy, contact the Voter News Service, 225 West 34th Street, Suite 310, New York, NY 10022. Telephone 212-947-7280; fax 212-947-7756. See also *USA Today,* April 12, 1993, p. 8A, "Gay Couples by the Numbers."
2. The Yankelovich MONITOR is an ongoing research project conducted annually (since 1971) by Yankelovich Partners. The underlying methodological assumption is that traditional economic and demographic predictors are insufficient for a complete understanding of marketplace behavior. In addition to measuring the traditional demographics, MONITOR is designed to quantitatively measure social attitudes, values and perceptions, thus sketching a complete portrait of the consumer.

▼ ▼

3. *Time*/CNN Poll, June 15–16, 1994, conducted by Yankelovich MONI-TOR, 101 Merritt 7 Corporate Park, Norwalk, CT 06851.
4. For more information on this trend, see Murdoch, *New York Times,* May 24, 1994, Section 4, p. 1.
5. See Susan Faludi, *Backlash: The Undeclared War Against Women* (New York: Crown, 1991).
6. *Life,* June 26, 1964, p. 76.
7. *Wall Street Journal,* May 13, 1975.

3: WHO IS THE GAY AND LESBIAN AMERICAN CONSUMER?

1. In Wardell B. Pomeroy, *Dr. Kinsey and the Institute for Sex Research* (New York: Harper & Row, 1972), p. 273.
2. In addition to the need for random probability sampling, there are other challenges to face when conducting research on sexual behavior and sexual identity in human beings. These include: making allowances for errors and distortions that can occur when respondents refuse to answer certain questions or withhold important information for undisclosed reasons; making allowances for participants who respond to questions the way they think they should, instead of expressing their understanding of the actual truth; or answering a question erroneously in response to what is perceived to be a trick question or one that could lead to criminal prosecution.

   All of these issues are faced by researchers, but they become especially important when conducting sexual research because of societal taboos about homosexuality, insecurity about one's own sexual behavior, or simply embarrassment over the discussion and consideration of the subject of sexuality itself. Therefore, it is nearly impossible to conduct a definitive study that will conclusively determine how many people are actually gay or lesbian.

   But sexual behavior alone does not determine sexual identity. What matters for marketing purposes is determining the number of individuals in a given geographic area who are willing to "self-identify" as being gay or lesbian—people who are willing to be counted as *"being gay or lesbian"* in a scientific study—regardless of their sexual behavior. By knowing this number first, marketers are provided with an extremely conservative estimate from which to make assumptions about the overall prospective marketplace and growth potentials.

   The point? Studies that cite sexual behavior tell us about just that—sexual behavior—which is radically different from consumer behavior. While it is true that some studies can arrive at general quantitative assumptions based on the consistency or exclusivity of people's sexual behavior, we are, again, only talking about sexual behavior. Segmenting advertising campaigns and marketing programs toward prospective gay

▼ ▼

and lesbian consumers requires more than relying on the same tired, scientifically quantified sexual behavior estimates cranked out by various universities and think tanks.

Behavioral studies telling us how many people are having what kind of sex in a given geographic area are of little importance or use to businesspeople wanting to make an honest buck with America's gay and lesbian consumer populations. Marketing studies that tell us how many people are willing to discuss their values, hopes, fears, wants, and needs while also self-identifying as being gay or lesbian tell us much more. Fortunately, more and more marketing studies based on gay and lesbian identity are now being conducted. Fewer and fewer behavioral studies on sexuality are being accepted as relevant to modern marketing science.

3. Lee Badgett, "The Wage Effect of Sexual Orientation Disemmination," *Industrial Labor Relations Review,* July 1995.

4. Rand's report to the U.S. Military (Contract No. MDA903-90-C-0004) was prepared for the Office of the Secretary of Defense (at the time, 1993, Les Aspin). It totaled over 500 pages and detailed major U.S. probability studies that were conducted under what Rand deemed sound scientific methodology. The Rand Corporation is a nonprofit institution that seeks to improve public policy through research and analysis. Rand publications do not necessarily reflect the opinions or policies of the sponsors of Rand research.

5. Pomeroy, *Dr. Kinsey and the Institute for Sex Research*, p. 3.

6. ———, p. 111.

7. ———, p. 112.

8. *Windy City Times,* April 8, 1993.

9. John O. Billy, et al., in *Family Planning Perspective* 25:52, published by the Alan Guttmacher Institute, 111 Fifth Avenue, New York, NY 10003.

10. The profile of the NGNG readership is the exclusive property of the National Gay Newspaper Guild. No use or quotation from the contents of this study may be made by anyone without the permission of a NGNG member or an authorized representative.

11. There has been some argument in academic circles over whether or not responses to inquiries are suppressed or elevated during sexual research interviews, particularly those dealing with issues of homosexuality. Some studies, like those cited in the Rand Report, use a self-administered questionnaire requiring the participant to divulge on paper the nature of their most intimate sexual feelings; other studies use face-to-face interviews, which still require participants to disclose verbally their sexual identity.

The Yankelovich technique is unique in that a spiral binder of fifty-

▼ ▼

two cards allows each respondent to simply flip through them and indicate only those card numbers that correspond to statements or words
that best describe them; one card is labeled gay/lesbian/homosexual.
This may seem only subtly different from choosing a box on an anonymous questionnaire or making a yes or no statement to an interviewer.
But as described in the previous chapter, when you consider the degree
to which most homosexual persons have either been a victim of, or are
familiar with, the way the church, the state, and the medical establishment have treated homosexuality, I argue that any respondent would
be suspicious of such a question no matter how it was put to them.

I believe the act of checking off a box on a questionnaire about
homosexuality has its own perceived implications in the subconscious
of the respondent—as would stating the fact verbally. The questionnaire leaves a paper trail; the face-to-face interview requires that the
respondent actually "state" his or her "orientation" or to say the word
gay or *lesbian* or *homosexual.* Subconsciously, many gay or lesbian
respondents might perceive the requirement to answer as a "confes-
sion" of what society has traditionally characterized as a "perversion,"
"sickness," or "crime" (whether they believed it was really an anonymous or confidential question or not).

Yankelovich's approach on this issue removes much more fear
from the respondent, allowing a greater comfort level with the divul-
gence of sexual identity. The respondent is not left with the feeling
that a "paper trail" has been left behind. I emphasize this issue
because a window of security has been provided through the spiral
binder approach, and that it has actually identified more gay and lesbian people in the population than previous, perhaps less sophisticated studies have indicated. In fact, it may be that—through this
process—some respondents actually acknowledged to themselves, for
the very first time, that they indeed are as the card indicated:
"gay/lesbian/homosexual."

4: Pride and Pragmatism: Understanding Gay and Lesbian Consumer Culture

1. Yankelovich MONITOR, 1994.
2. National Public Radio, "All Things Considered," January 16, 1994.
3. *New York Times,* Tuesday, May 30, 1995, page A5.
4. Issued May 30, 1995.
5. Mark Thompson, *Gay Soul: Interviews and Photographs* (San Francisco: HarperSanFrancisco, 1994).
6. Timothy J. Gilfoyle, *City of Eros: New York City, Prosititution, and the Commercialization of Sex, 1790–1920* (New York: W.W. Norton, 1992), pp. 19, 30, 98–99, 254.

▼ ▼

7. ———, pp. 98–99.
8. John D'Emilio, *Sexual Politics, Sexual Communities: The Making of a Homosexual Minority in the United States, 1940–1970* (Chicago: University of Chicago Press, 1983), pp. 19, 247.
9. The specific discussion of exactly what the Yankelovich data means has been formulated by and, in some cases, taken verbatim from Yankelovich Partners research reports. The theory of the *psychology of disenfranchisement*, presented at this chapter's end, is based on the personal theories and writings of Yankelovich researcher Rex Briggs. However, the arguments made, social parallels drawn, and questions raised *in relation* to the data's meaning throughout the rest of this book, are solely the author's unless otherwise noted.
10. From the "Social Climate Overview" section of the 1993 and 1994 Yankelovich MONITOR. This material is intended to provide a broad contextual understanding of the total population. It is part of a focused analysis of the gay/lesbian population in the Yankelovich MONITOR Gay and Lesbian Perspective.
11. Lee Badgett, "The Wage Effect of Sexual Orientation Discrimination," *Industrial Labor Relations Review,* July 1995.

    See also Badgett, Colleen Donnelly, and Jennifer Kibbe, "Pervasive Patterns of Discrimination Against Lesbians and Gay Men: Evidence from Surveys Across the United States," National Gay and Lesbian Task Force Policy Institute, 1992; and Thomas A. Stewart, "Gay in Corporate America," *Fortune,* Dec. 1, 1991.

5: BRAND LOYALTY, MANAGEMENT, AND CREATIVE PROCESS: PROMOTING PRODUCTS AND SERVICES TO GAY AND LESBIAN CONSUMERS

1. Faith Popcorn, *The Popcorn Report: Faith Popcorn on the Future of Your Company, Your World, Your Life* (New York: HarperBusiness, 1992), p. 162.
2. The Wall Street Project's Equality Principles on Sexual Orientation:

    1. Explicit prohibitions against discrimination based on sexual orientation will be included in the company's written employment policy statement.
    2. Discrimination against HIV-positive employees or those with AIDS will be strictly prohibited.
    3. Employee groups, regardless of sexual orientation, will be given equal standing with other employee associations.
    4. Diversity training will include sexual orientation issues.
    5. Spousal benefits will be offered to domestic partners of employees, regardless of sexual orientation, on an equal basis with those granted to married employees.

▼ ▼

6. Company advertising policy will bar negative sexual orientation stereotypes and will not discriminate in media advertising on the basis of sexual orientation.

7. Companies will not discriminate in the sale and purchase of goods and services on the basis of sexual orientation.

8. Written nondiscrimination policies on sexual orientation must be disseminated throughout the company. A senior company official will monitor compliance corporate wide.

3. Ed Mickens, "Waging War on Wall Street," *The Advocate,* April 19, 1994, p. 41.

4. *The Nation,* April 15, 1978, p. 434.

5. Russ Bellant, *The Coors Connection: How Coors Family Philanthropy Undermines Democratic Pluralism* (Boston: South End Press, 1988).

6. *Time,* December 2, 1977. See also, for example, sworn statement of Richard Anderson, Sept. 28, 1977; sworn statement of John Kincannon, Sept. 20, 1977.

7. This information is available from the National Gay and Lesbian Task Force and is also chronicled in two important books, *Cracking the Corporate Closet* and *The One Hundred Best Companies for Gay Men and Lesbians* (see bibliography).

8. See Cohen, Dorothy. *Consumer Behavior* (New York: Random House Business, 1981), p. 207.

9. " No Time for Miller Time," *Outweek,* August 22, 1990.

10. *Wall Street Journal,* May 13, 1975.

6: RAINBOW TARGET MARKETING: INSIGHTS AND OPPORTUNITIES FOR BUSINESS

1. *New York Times,* September 6, 1994.

2. *Frontiers* magazine, May 19, 1995.

3. The New York Advertising and Communications Network is part of the Network of Business and Professional Organizations, Inc.

4. See Cracker Barrel discussion in Chapter 5.

7: THE FUTURE OF THE GAY AND LESBIAN MARKETPLACE: CONSIDERATIONS AT THE DOOR OF THE TWENTY-FIRST CENTURY

1. *Advertising Age,* May 2, 1994.

2. *Wall Street Journal,* March 15, 1994.

3. *New York Times,* December 1, 1993 (in the Media Business column, Elliott).

4. *New York Times,* June 11, 1993.

SELECTED BIBLIOGRAPHY

▼▼▼▼▼▼▼▼▼▼▼▼▼▼▼▼▼▼▼▼▼▼▼▼▼▼

Altman, Dennis. *The Homosexualization of America, The Americanization of the Homosexual.* New York: St. Martin's Press, 1982.

Baker, Daniel, Sean O'Brien Strub, and Bill Henning. *Cracking the Corporate Closet.* New York: HarperBusiness, 1995.

Bawer, Bruce. *A Place at the Table.* New York: Poseidon Press, 1993.

Bellant, Russ. *The Coors Connection: How Coors Family Philanthropy Undermines Democratic Pluralism.* Boston: South End Press, 1988.

Berube, Allan. *Coming Out Under Fire: The History of Gay Men and Women in World War Two.* New York: Free Press, 1990.

Boswell, John. *Christianity, Social Tolerance, and Homosexuality: Gay People in Western Europe from the Beginning of the Christian Era to the Fourteenth Century.* Chicago: University of Chicago Press, 1980.

Browning, Frank. *The Culture of Desire: Paradox and Perversity in Gay Lives Today.* New York: Crown, 1993.

Chauncey, George. *Gay New York: Gender, Urban Culture, and the Making of the Gay Male World, 1890–1940.* New York: HarperCollins 1994.

Chilton, John. *Billie's Blues: The Billie Holiday Story.* Chelsea, MI: Scarborough House, 1975.

Cohen, Dorothy. *Consumer Behavior.* New York: Random House, 1981.

D'Emilio, John. *Sexual Politics, Sexual Communities: The Making of a Homosexual Minority in the United States, 1940–1970.* Chicago: University of Chicago Press, 1983.

D'Emilio, John, and Estelle B. Freedman. *Intimate Matters: A History of Sexuality in America.* New York: Harper & Row, 1988.

Duberman, Martin. *Stonewall.* New York: Dutton, 1993.

Duberman, Martin, Martha Vicinus, and George Chauncey, Jr. *Hidden from History: Reclaiming the Gay and Lesbian Past.* New York: Penguin, 1989.

Faludi, Susan. *Backlash: The Undeclared War Against Women.* New York: Crown, 1991.

Gentry, Curt. *J. Edgar Hoover: The Man and the Secrets.* New York: W.W. Norton, 1991.

Gilfoyle, Timothy J. *City of Eros: New York City, Prostitution, and the Commercialization of Sex, 1790–1920.* New York: W.W. Norton, 1992.

Gore, Al. *Earth in the Balance: Ecology and the Human Spirit.* Boston: Houghton Mifflin, 1992

195

▼ ▼

Grun, Bernard. *The Timetables of History: A Horizontal Linkage of People and Events.* 3rd revised edition. New York: Touchstone, 1991. Based upon Werner Stein's *Kulturfahrplan.*

Hammer, Michael, and James Champy. *Reengineering the Corporation: A Manifesto for Business Revolution.* New York: HarperBusiness, 1993.

Handlin, Oscar, and Mary F. Handlin. *The Wealth of the American People.* New York: McGraw Hill, 1975.

Hofstader & Miller. *The United States.* New York: Prentice Hall, 1972.

Holiday, Billie, and William F. Dufty. *Lady Sings the Blues.* New York: Doubleday, 1956.

James, Burnett. *Billie Holiday: Nineteen Fifteen to Nineteen Fifty-five.* New York: Hippocrene Books, 1984.

Johnson, Otto, exec. ed. *The 1994 Information Please Almanac.* Boston: Houghton Mifflin, 1994.

Katz, Jonathan. *Gay American History: Lesbians and Gay Men in the U.S.A.* New York: Crowell, 1976.

———. *The Invention of Heterosexuality.* New York: Penguin, 1995.

Kaufman, Louis. *Essentials of Advertising.* San Diego: Harcourt Brace Jovanovich, 1980.

Kearney, Elizabeth I., and Michale J. Bandley. *People Power: Reading People For Results.* Provo, UT: Community Press, 1990.

———. *Customers Run Your Company: They Pay The Bills!* Provo, UT: Community Press, 1990.

Larson, Erik. *The Naked Consumer: How Our Private Lives Become Public Commodities.* New York: Henry Holt, 1992.

Lieb, Sandra R. *Mother of the Blues: A Study of Ma Rainey.* Amherst: University of Massachusetts Press, 1981.

Marsh, Dave. *Fifty Ways to Fight Censorship.* New York: Thunder's Mouth, 1991.

Mickens, Ed. *The 100 Best Companies for Gay Men and Lesbians.* New York: Pocket Books, 1994.

Miller, Alice. *Breaking Down the Wall of Silence: The Liberating Experience of Facing the Painful Truth.* New York: Dutton, 1991.

Nussbaum, Bruce. *Good Intentions: How Big Business and the Medical Establishment Are Corrupting the Fight Against AIDS.* New York: Atlantic Montlhy Press, 1990.

Oliver, Paul. *Bessie Smith.* New York: A.S. Barnes, 1959.

Paglia, Camille. *Sex, Art, and American Culture.* New York: Vintage, 1992.

Pomeroy, Wardell B. *Dr. Kinsey and the Institue for Sex Research.* New York: Harper and Row, 1972.

Popcorn, Faith. *The Popcorn Report: Faith Popcorn on the Future of Your Company, Your World, Your Life.* New York: HarperBusiness, 1992.

Posener, Jill. *Spray It Loud.* New York: Routledge and Kegan Paul, 1982.

Rampersad, Arnold. *The Life of Langston Hughes*. New York: Oxford University Press, 1986.

Rector, Frank. *The Nazi Extermination of Homosexuals*. Briarcliff Manor, NY: Stein and Day, 1981.

Roberts, Mary L., and Paul D. Berger. *Direct Marketing Management*. New York: Prentice Hall, 1989.

Rutledge, Leigh W. *The Gay Decades: From Stonewall to the Present—The People and Events That Shaped Gay Lives*. New York: Dutton, 1992.

Rutten, Peter, Albert F. Bayers III, and Kelly Maloni. *Net Guide: Your Map to the Services, Information and Entertainment on the Electronic Highway*. New York: Random House Electronic Publishing, 1994.

Sante, Luc. *Low Life: Lures and Snares of Old New York*. New York: Vintage, 1991.

Shilts, Randy. *Conduct Unbecoming: Gays and Lesbians in the U.S. Military*. New York: St. Martin's Press, 1993.

Signorile, Michaelangelo. *Queer in America: Sex, the Media, and the Closets of Power*. New York: Random House, 1993.

Summers, Anthony. *Official and Confidential: The Secret Life of J. Edgar Hoover*. New York: Putnam, 1993.

Tannahill, Reay. *Sex in History*. Briarcliff Manor, NY: Stein and Day, 1980.

Thompson, Mark. *Gay Soul: Interviews and Photographs*. San Francisco: HarperSanFrancisco, 1994.

Von Hoffman, Nicholas. *Citizen Cohn: The Life and Times of Roy Cohn*. New York: Doubleday, 1988.

West, Cornel. *Race Matters*. Boston: Beacon Press, 1993.

INDEX

▼ ▼

▼ ▼

▼ ▼

▼ ▼

▼ ▼

▼ ▼

▼ ▼

▼ ▼